Tobacco

AN EXPLORATION OF ITS NATURE THROUGH THE PRISM OF HOMEOPATHY

Tobacco

AN EXPLORATION OF ITS NATURE THROUGH THE PRISM OF HOMEOPATHY

Richard Pitt

LALIBELA PUBLISHING

Book and cover design: 13^2 Studio

Lalibela Publishing
1199 Sanchez Street
San Francisco, CA 94114

Nicotiana rustica

May the scent of the Tobacco
I have thrown on the Sacred Fire
Reach Thee, Creator Father, to let Thee know
We are still good and that thou mayest give us
All that we have asked.

Iroquois Prayer

Those human cultures which demonize
death or pain or sickness are thus less able to deal
with the bitter side of nature, with intoxications;
and make themselves doubly sick.

Gary Snyder

A cigarette is the perfect type of a perfect pleasure.
It is exquisite and it leaves one unsatisfied.
What more can one want?

Oscar Wilde

I believe that pipe smoking contributes to a somewhat calm
and objective judgment in all human affairs.

Albert Einstein

Contents

Acknowledgements

I would like to thank all the provers and supervisors who made this proving possible. The provers were students at the Pacific Academy of Homeopathy, San Francisco, The Homeopathic Academy of Southern California, and the Vancouver Academy of Homeopathy, Vancouver, BC. I specifically would like to thank Allison Maslan from San Diego for her work in coordinating and evaluating the provers from her school. I would like to express great appreciation to Jenny Decker, student of the Pacific Academy, for all her work in compiling the proving material and for researching the correlations between Native American uses of tobacco and the proving. I want to acknowledge the support of Corey, Mary, Caroline, Kathy and John, my co-workers, and to thank my partner, Lyn and her daughter Julia, who supported me in so many ways in this venture and others. I also want to thank John Morgan of Helios Pharmacy, at whose house the original idea of this proving came to light, and who has been a comrade in the homeopathic trenches for many years, and to Alice Duncan, friend and editor, whose skills have made such a difference to this project. Thanks also to my old friend Jo Daly who supplied the excellent case of Tabacum for the book. Finally, I want to thank Heidi Schor and especially to Karen Schwartz who did a tremendous job to get the material into shape when it really mattered—right at the end. And really finally, I would like to thank Mirna and Missy of 13^2 Studio, my favorite graphic artists, who performed the most important task with such dedication—to make it look so pleasing to the eye.

Preface

Like Cures Like. What can cause illness can cure illness. One man's poison is another man's medicine.

In homeopathic medicine, the journey begins by exploring the healing power of nature, to understand its potential to heal. This is done through provings. A proving is an experimental and experiential process where people ingest small doses of substances to see what it will do to them, to experience their effect on mind and body. Through this experience, an image is created, an impression made. The collective experience of people taking a substance becomes the picture of the effect of a substance when given to healthy people. This then becomes the information of what this substance can cure in a person who is sick. Like Cures Like. A substance that can create symptoms in healthy people will cure *similar* symptoms in a person who is sick. That is the basis of homeopathy. *Similia Similibus Curentur,* as its stated in Latin. In homeopathy it is termed a Law of Cure, a biological mechanism through which the body's own innate ability to heal is stimulated. Cure occurs when the body heals itself. All holistic therapies work on this premise, including homeopathy.

Introduction

A homeopathic proving is one of the most profound ways to find out about the essential nature of a substance. The proving substance allows us to explore the "consciousness" of a substance—be it plant, animal or mineral—and reveals the potential to its healing power through the physical and psychological experiences of each prover. Every substance in nature is unique, and the relationship between humans and the proving material offers a great amount of information and knowledge about both the substance and human beings.

One of the most essential aspects of a homeopathic proving is its experiential nature. It is an immediate empirical process, a journey into the essence of the substance. However, in order for a proving to help us understand the full spectrum of a substance, that substance has to be taken by as large number of people as possible. One prover's response cannot reveal all there is to see in any substance. Likewise, a substance needs to be given in a number of homeopathic potencies to reveal a more complete remedy picture.

The complete healing potential of a substance can only be seen and confirmed in clinical practice. The challenge involved in a proving is therefore to accurately analyze and apply the information derived from the proving to the treatment of real patients in clinical situations.

Another way to find out about the "nature" of a substance is to study it in its natural (unpotentized) form and observe its impact on the world of nature and human activity. Nearly every substance interacts with or influences humans in some way, and many are used for practical and economic benefit. Information about these interactions can also give us insight about the nature of a substance and its possible clinical effects. Considering that every characteristic may be an expression of some quality or facet of the whole, interesting—or even essential—information about a substance can be gleaned in many ways.

Given that a homeopathic proving is a means of exploring the healing power of a substance that has been ingested in some form by human beings, the knowledge gained through this method can be usefully compared to knowledge about the substance gained from other sources. The relative importance of possible therapeutic information taken from sources outside of provings is a matter of contention in homeopathic thinking. Some homeopaths are inclined to dismiss the significance of any information that does not come directly from provings, adhering to the idea that only information gleaned directly from provings is acceptable. However, as is well known to those who have been involved with provings, the challenge of extracting authentic remedy information from such a large amount of subjective material can be difficult, as can be seen in some of the original provings of Samuel Hahnemann, the founder of homeopathy, as well as in some provings conducted in modern times.

Therefore, if it is possible to study correspondences between provings and other more "observational" phenomena, this may add to our knowledge of the substance and its homeopathic affinity. It should be kept in mind, however, that the homeopathic healing potential of a substance can only be reliably verified by clinical results.

The chapters that follow—before the information from the proving is presented—will explore the substance Nicotiana rustica from many different angles. A brief overview of botanical and pharmacological aspects of tobacco is given, followed by a more detailed story of the relationship between humans and tobacco. Considering the extraordinary impact tobacco has had on human civilizations, it seems worthwhile to explore this history, even if it is not directly connected to the proving. The next chapter highlights the comparison between tobacco and other homeopathic remedies, including an elucidation of some of the main themes from the proving. A deeper look at some of the symptoms, thoughts, and feelings arising during the proving is then explored and compared with experiences by Native Americans who have used tobacco. This is followed by the complete picture of the proving, accompanied by the repertorization of the proving, as well as a case in which the remedy Tabacum was given.

The information in this book is by no means a complete description of the remedy-picture of Nicotiana rustica. It would be interesting to conduct future provings using even higher potencies. The presentation of this material is, however, an attempt to use the foundation of a homeopathic proving as a means to study one of the most intriguing substances known to humans, which has had a significant impact on the history, lives, and consciousness of human beings.

Chapter One

The Substance, the Process and Its Human Connection

The idea of conducting a homeopathic proving of Nicotiana rustica was inspired, in part, by reading Jeremy Narby's book, *The Cosmic Serpent,* which explores experiences with the indigenous plant Ayahuasca by Shamans of South America's Amazon region. Tobacco is also used by the people of this region and is one of the substances allied with Ayahuasca and used as a tool in their purification ceremonies and explorations of other states of consciousness. The form of tobacco used is Nicotiana rustica, which is closely related to Nicotiana tabacum (which is potentized to make the remedy Tabacum), the two being the only two cultivated species of tobacco. The main distinction is that N. rustica has approximately four times the nicotine that N. tabacum contains. Although Tabacum is a well-known remedy in homeopathy, its picture is incomplete, especially in its psychological aspects.

Therefore, a proving of a different botanical form of tobacco with greater concentration of nicotine might bring out more themes and symptoms for the study of tobacco-related remedies. Also, given the extraordinary history of the use of tobacco by human beings, and the current cultural "war" against tobacco, its significance as a homeopathic remedy has perhaps not been completely understood.

The Botany and Pharmacology of Tobacco

Tobacco is a member of the Solanaceae family. There are two cultivated species of tobacco, Nicotiana tabacum and Nicotiana rustica. Both of these species are tetraploids, the result of a fertile hybrid between two wild species at some time in antiquity, evidently in the Andean region of South America. Almost all American and European commercial tobaccos are Nicotiana tabacum. There are some five dozen wild species of Nicotiana, three-quarters of them native to the Americas. These species include N. glauca, N. sylvestris, N. trigonophylla, N. attenuata, N. bigelovii, and N. petuniodes. Nicotine content is highest in the cultivated species, and is much higher in Nicotiana rustica than in Nicotiana tabacum.[1]

Nicotine is the key alkaloid found in tobacco. Extremely addictive and poisonous, one or two drops of pure nicotine can be lethal. In some varieties of Nicotiana rustica, the nicotine content of the leaves can be as high as 20 percent. Nicotine is structurally similar to acetylcholine, a neurotransmitter active in both the sympathetic and parasympathetic nervous systems, as well as in the somatic nervous system at neuromuscular junctures. Research has shown that acetylcholine is present in the Central Nervous System (CNS), which gives some neurochemical support for findings that nicotine affects learning. In the CNS, nicotine increases arousal and enhances the learning and performance of simple tasks. Nicotine can act as either a stimulant or a sedative, depending on the amount taken. Nicotine's parasympathetic stimulation of the smooth muscles of the digestive tract has been understood for some time. Its actions on the sympathetic nervous system are less well-known, but, in addition to its mimicking of acetycholine, nicotine also stimulates the release of epinephrine (adrenalin) and dopamine, and in smaller amounts, norepinephrine and serotonin. Norepinephrine is a neurohormone chemically related to mescaline. The significance of these neurotransmitters to the alleged hallucinatory effects of tobacco is still inconclusive, although N. rustica contains the alkaloid harmaline, absent in N. tabacum, which has been demonstrated to potentiate the psychoactive properties of other alkaloids. Toxic effects of tobacco include perspiration, lightheadedness, general weakness, tremors, convulsions and respiratory paralysis.[2]

Tobacco's connection to other psychoactive substances was explored during research into the effects of Ayahuasca when toxicologists extracted the active compound from the Banisteriopsis vine from which Ayahuasca is made, naming it Telepathine. In 1957 researchers discovered that Telepathine was actually Harmine, one of several compounds from the beta-carboline family of hallucinogens. Secondary alkaloids called Harmaline and Tetrahydroharmine were also identified.

The action of nicotine on the brain is now being explored in regard to the treatment of Alzheimer's disease. It could be that the harmaline alkaloid found in tobacco is involved in part of that action on the brain. Nicotine acts on the nicotinic receptors for acetylcholine, which exist in the brain as well as in the rest of the body.

Several brain-areas that can be affected by Alzheimer's disease contain nicotinic receptors for acetylcholine, but the number of these receptors seems to be greatly reduced in Alzheimer's disease patients. If nicotinic receptors are blocked in normal people by drugs such as mecamylamine, the subjects do not perform as well in learning and reasoning tests. Conversely, the receptors can be activated by nicotine itself, and tests in animals and humans show that nicotine increases the ability of patients to pay attention to events and to remember new things. Smokers, of course, will not be surprised by this, as it has long been claimed that alertness, attention, memory, and thinking are enhanced by smoking. Nicotine patches are now being developed for use in Alzheimer's disease, to help the mental condition without the serious health problems that accompany smoking. Because nicotine activates receptors in the muscles, intestines and nerves, leading to digestive and cardiovascular problems, several companies are developing drugs that activate the nicotinic receptors in the brain only.

Ayahuasca, Tobacco and DNA – The Mother, The Son and the Holy Ghost

In *The Cosmic Serpent*, Jeremy Narby describes how his work as an anthropologist in Brazil led him to experience many divergent uses of tobacco. One man used tobacco as a healing agent, blowing smoke onto a sick child. The man said that Ayahuasca had led them to the use of tobacco. Ayahuasca is often called the mother, whereas Tobacco is the child. Both Ayahuasca and Tobacco attract the spirits (souls). "Souls like tobacco... because tobacco has its method, its strength. It attracts the maninkari (invisible beings/spirits). It is the best contact for the life of a human being."[3]

Amongst the people of the Amazon, the belief in spirits as real phenomena is common, but so is the awareness that contact with spirits gives power not only to cure but to harm. Not all societies and Shamans in the Amazon use hallucinogens, but in Western Amazonia, which includes the Peruvian, Ecuadorian and Columbian part of the basin, it is hard to find a culture that does not use psychoactive plants. According to one inventory, there are 72 Ayahuasca-using cultures in Western Amazonia.

"Civilized" people have been extraordinarily reluctant to accept that plants can communicate knowledge to human beings through their ingestion. In his 2001 book *The Botany of Desire,* Michael Pollan discussed the idea that every plant contains a level of knowledge about both the plant and the wider world that is communicable to humans on a conscious level. Pollan describes relationships between plants and humans, such as how Cannabis indica "uses" us for its own survival and evolution as much as we use the plant. The idea that hallucinations can be a source of real information and can communicate like human beings is not endorsed in conventional scientific circles, to say the least. Outside of indigenous cultures that use hallucinogenic plants and subcultures in western societies influenced through the use of LSD and other psychedelics, the conclusions drawn by these cultures are rejected. However, communication from plant to human remains an open question. As Narby writes, "The enigma of hallucinatory knowledge could be reduced to one question: Was this information coming from *inside* the human brain, as the scientific point of view would have it, or from the *outside* world of plants, as shamans claim?"[4]

From a homeopathic point of view, the answer would be that the information derives from both sources, but primarily the latter.

We are exploring the consciousness of nature when doing a proving, each substance having a unique identity and message. However, all human beings participating in a proving also connect to the substance on the level of their own susceptibilities, reflecting something inherent in each of them. Narby came to a similar conclusion.

The main thrust of Narby's book is that ingesting hallucinogens such as Ayahuasca actually connects a person to the DNA level of reality. All living things share a similar DNA pattern, the difference between a cockroach and a human being much less than we would like to think. Therefore, on a DNA level, ALL living things are connected. As Narby says, "the molecule of life is the same for all species and the genetic information in a rose, a bacterium, or a human being is coded in a universal language of four letters, A, G, C and T, which are four chemical compounds contained in a DNA double helix."[5] Consequently, the knowledge is within us and merely has to be accessed. Taking hallucinogenic drugs or doing homeopathic provings is a way to communicate through DNA patterns. Narby conceptually connects the images of snakes, serpents and other reptiles that are often experienced by ingesting Ayahuasca to the structure of DNA molecules and the double helix formation. His exploration showed that different tribes and cultures shared similar experiences in using Ayahuasca, and the cosmologies seen were connected to their experience with the substance. Narby concluded that the connections were not coincidental but part of a more universal experience. In pre-Christian times, serpents symbolized creation and creator gods, a symbolism common to many cultures throughout the world. Narby comments:

> The visible snake appears as merely the brief incarnation of a Great Invisible Serpent, which is causal and timeless, a master of the vital principle and of all the forces of nature. It is a primary old god found at the beginning of all cosmogonies, before monotheism and reason toppled it. [6]

However, in both ancient Greek and later Christian times the serpent came to represent evil, with Yahweh defeating the serpent of the cosmic sea, Leviathian. To illustrate the significance of this symbolic change in the image of the serpent Narby makes reference to Joseph Campbell:

> Meanwhile the damnation of the serpent is particularly ambiguous; Yahweh accuses it of having shown Eve the tree that allows one to tell the difference between good and evil; how can one apply the Ten Commandments without an understanding of this difference? According to Campbell, these patriarchal inversions "address a pictorial message to the heart that exactly reverses the verbal message addressed to the brain; and this nervous discord inhabits both Christianity and Islam as well as Judaism, since they too share the legacy of the Old Testament."[7]

This concept of good and evil is central to Judeo-Christian thinking as well as Islam, representing itself in contrasting images of dark and light and in psychological terms of the conscious and unconscious processes, the id and the ego. Interestingly, in homeopathy the remedies from the Solanaceae family clearly reflect this polarity, and along with the snake remedies used in homeopathy such as Lachesis (surucucu) and Crotalus Horridus (rattlesnake), express language of being divided, split, with a fear of the unknown – the dark, demons, ghosts, violence, etc, suppressed fears seeking a form of conscious expression.

This polarity of good and evil can be seen in the proving of Nicotiana rustica. The original proving and toxicology of Tabacum revealed less of this polarity than did provings of other Solanaceae, especially Stramonium and Belladonna. It can therefore be seen that the action of Solanaceae remedies is to bring together these two parts, to shine light onto darkness and vice versa, to accept both sides of the equation.

Another thread in this reasoning is revealed by exploring what homeopathic provings actually do. By experiencing the consciousness of a plant, mineral or animal, humans also experience the revelation that we are not the center of the world in which we live. The illusion of the centrality of human experience in the world is discussed in a fascinating way in John Gray's book, *Straw Dogs*. In doing a proving, this illusion begins to crumble, and the assumption (put forth by the ancient Greeks and hallowed by Judeo-Christian doctrine) that humans represent the highest flowering of evolutionary consciousness comes to look increasingly fallacious. We are but one part of the web of consciousness of the planet. All things can be said to have a soul, even non-living forms. A homeopathic proving is a way to connect to this level of consciousness. Provings are therefore one way of experiencing the reality of the universe beyond the immediate human one, while signifying our connection to it.

The Consciousness Between Man, Tobacco and the Spirit World

Every culture has its own drugs. They are used in many ways—as a sacrament, a spiritual journey, a medicine, an indulgence and an addiction. There is no consistency as to which substances are chosen. Generally a few substances are chosen and others are avoided and even demonized. Tobacco has historically been more successful than most in ingratiating itself into different cultures and only now is it finding itself on the defensive, mainly in western societies. Is that due to its nature or the way in which humans have used and abused it? This is one of the things that is being explored in this book—how the consciousness of a culture alters their relationship to drugs and to nature itself. How has the relationship between tobacco and the "White Man" differed from that of indigenous societies. Have we in the West merely resorted to seeing tobacco as a form of economic enterprise and addictive substance, mixing it with toxins which then poisons our body without any understanding of its real nature? Do all indigenous cultures have a much more benign and evolved understanding of tobacco and its usage? That is a fair conclusion if one looks at modern history (the last 500 years) but as with most things, it may not always be the case.

In the northern Amazonia, on the borders of Brazil, Columbia and Venezuela, there are two tribes, the Tucano and the Yanomamo, whose use of tobacco is somewhat different, along with their use of other indigenous plants. The Tucano people generally use Tobacco as spiritual guide, and it is mostly taken by smoking, whereas the

Yanomamo people generally use Tobacco purely for enjoyment and addiction. They mostly imbibe it through chewing. One other difference is that the Tucano people use Ayahuasca or Yage as an integral part of their spiritual journey, whereas the Yanomamo culture use Ebene, a snuff made from the seeds of the Anadenanthera species, or the inner bark of the Virola species. While both have hallucinogenic properties, the effect of Ayahuasca is to create a much stronger disassociative effect in which the practitioner can seemingly experience other states of reality outside of their immediate one. It is akin to the feeling of soul travel, and Ayahuasca is called "Vine of the soul." Chemically, this is due to the fact that the Ayahuasca mixture contains a beta-carboline monamine oxidase inhibitor that renders N,N-dimethyltryptamine (DMT) orally active and delays its metabolization. Tobacco is used by the Tucano people to enhance the hallucinogenic effect of Ayahuasca and has been mentioned, Nicotiana rustica contains small amounts of harmine (a beta-carboline) which has a hallucinogenic effect. The use of Ebene by the Yanomamo people does not produce such a strong effect and they do not use tobacco in the same way that the Tucano people do.

Correspondingly, both tribes have a different view of the spiritual world and their relationship to it. The Tucano believe that their ancestors live on a different plane of existence which tobacco and Ayahuasca transports them to. The Yanomamo believe that when they die they go to live again on another plane. They don't believe that they can contact ancestors and other departed souls on other planes. They believe that certain spirits can come and enter Shamans and with the powers this gives the Shaman may use it for good or for harm. Ebene is the tool they used to contact these spirits and to try and keep them happy. Therefore the Tucano have a more externalized view of the universe and their relationship to it, whereas the Yanomamo have a more internalized view. Even the way tobacco is used expresses this different view. The Tucano smoke—often giant cigars—and do so in a ceremonial way and for purification, as well as enhancing the effect of Ayahuasca. The very process of smoking, inhaling and then exhaling volumes of smoke further emphasizes the connection between different worlds, a theme seen repeatedly with tobacco use by many cultures, woven into symbology, and also seen in the homeopathic proving. The Yanomamo mainly chew tobacco, swallowing the juices in a more internal process, and they partake of tobacco in much more habitual way, similar to their use of Ebene. Ebene is taken by putting powder in a long hollow tube and a man forcibly blows it into another man's nostrils. It is used more recreationally than is Ayahuasca, similar to how the different forms of tobacco have been used, the tamer fire of Nicotiana tabacum suiting repeated use in comparison to the more stimulative and mind altering effects of Nicotiana rustica.

The many ways in which tobacco has been used is explored in the following chapter, comparing the traditional uses of tobacco by native peoples to that of the Europeans and white settlers of the Americas. There is no doubt that the method of taking in tobacco is a significant factor in understanding its effect. Chewing tobacco has a relentless quality to it, more physical and pragmatic than the smoking of huge cigars with voluminous smoke creating an "otherworldly" effect and different again to the smoking of narrow cigarettes, which are sucked intensely into the depths of the body, internalizing the smoke and the emotions with it, before being reluctantly exhaled. All methods of partaking of tobacco has to reflect the consciousness for taking the poison into the body in the first place.

Similar to the internalized spiritual consciousness of the Yanomamo and the use of tobacco as a daily habit and addiction, the white man has used tobacco in a similar way. Not attracted to the stronger physical and psychological effect of Nicotiana rustica, the first American settlers were able to cultivate a milder smoke, Nicotiana tabacum, its mildly stimulative effect suiting better the mental and physical characteristics of European people. Perhaps the views of the Yanomamo and the Europeans regarding a more internalized spiritual view were similar, leading to a similar relationship to tobacco. The Europeans had an externalized god, but a god that was not directly accessible. Other realities of consciousness and the ability to connect to these realities were taboo, the history of witch burning in Europe a testament to the prevailing fears of the unknown and evil, all dark forces to be avoided and purged. Even today, 500 years later, similar views prevail in many parts of the "developed" world. Perhaps because hallucinogens similar to Ayahuasca were not so widely used in European culture (certain mushrooms and types of alcohol being the closest), there was not so much opportunity to explore other levels of consciousness, and the power of the Church firmly controlled the conscious imagination, demonizing all things unknown and keeping man separate from the world in which he lived.

So, the use of tobacco—taken on its own and with other substances—has always been seen as a form of communication - between peoples, cultures and different worlds, a connection between temporal and spiritual realities. If the relationship to other realities and worlds is one of fear, then perhaps the energy of tobacco is taken inward, whereas if the consciousness of other worlds is more inclusive, then the energy of tobacco can be transported outward. As with any substance, tobacco has many facets.

Chapter Two

A Brief History of Tobacco

THE EARLY YEARS

Nicotiana rustica and Nicotiana tabacum are native to the Americas. The first time people came across them was probably about 18,000 years ago. These peoples are thought to have originated from Asia, coming to the Americas via the Bering Straits, which at that time had a land bridge. Gradually, they made use of many plants, including tobacco. It has been established that tobacco's place of origin was the Peruvian/Ecuadorian Andes, and its first cultivation occurred some time between 5,000-3,000 BC. It spread from there throughout the American continent, north and south. How tobacco was first used is not clear but is likely to have been the practice of sniffing powdered tobacco up the nose. Snuff-taking became one of the most popular forms of tobacco ingestion until the first decades of the 20th century when cigarettes became more commonly used, especially after the 1st world war, when tobacco became "man's best friend."

Tobacco was widely used from the earliest time, being smoked, chewed, sniffed, eaten, drunk, and smeared over bodies. It was blown into warrior's faces before battle, over women prior to sex and given as an offering to the gods. It became a very versatile part of human activity. Even in the early days of plant cultivation, tobacco was used as an insecticide, smoke being blown over plants and tobacco juice plastered over the skin to kill parasites. Tobacco has also been used to symbolize the process of becoming a man, from the times of the earliest tribes and their rituals, to the present day when a teenager's foray's into tobacco represent a coming of age, of being seen as grown up and tough.

It's role as medicine has always been an important part of tobacco use, especially by South American societies who were the first people to use tobacco. It would be given for toothaches, snake-bite and various other conditions. Most importantly, it was used to overcome their spiritual afflictions, which were thought to be caused by supernatural forces. Tobacco became a vital part of the training of the shamans who were the healers of such spiritual maladies. Shamans often ingested so much tobacco they approached the point of death, in an attempt to develop the powers to address such profound and life threatening problems. Tobacco was often chewed, so much larger quantities could be taken in, as well as drunk in the form of tea where the doses could be adjusted. Tobacco "tea" would also be taken via the anus in an enema and also sniffed up the nose. Often tobacco and other substances such as coca would be sniffed together. Tobacco was used with hashish or ganga, an ally in the process of changing consciousness. The Inca people were particularly fond of sniffing tobacco. Smoking was a favorite way of taking tobacco, both for ceremonial use and for everyday indulgence. Huge cigars were common, helpful to alleviate hunger and given as presents and expressions of friendship. The Mayan civilization that inhabited Central America between about 2000BC and 900AD used tobacco extensively, both for ritual and for pleasure. The Aztecs, who lived in what is now Mexico, also used it as a ritual and as medicine, as well as for enjoyment. The Aztecs were an imperial people, known for human sacrifice, where tobacco was as an accompaniment to this practice. Tobacco smoke was blown over warriors before battle, an early example of the connection between tobacco and war and death.

Tobacco was also used in North America prior to 2500BC. Some of the earliest tribes, living nomadic lives, still took time to cultivate tobacco; it seems, in fact, to have been the only plant they cultivated. This is another example of the unique intimacy between humans and tobacco. Archeological evidence of early tribes shows that tobacco use was common and that the tobacco pipe was a favorite object of these people. Ornate individualized pipes were often buried with a person, and pipes were a crucial part of a person's possessions. To quote from the book, *La Diva Nicotina – The Story of How Tobacco Seduced The World,* by Iain Gately:

> "These pipes were for personal use: when an individual wished to communicate with his totem, or the spirit world, he would smoke his tobacco pipe, which had been shaped to represent his totemic animal or a recognized messenger with the spirits. Smoking appears to have been a form of profound meditation—a device to raise the smoker above the distractions of a world of flesh. As a smoker inhaled he literally drank the substance of the eternal, and the smoke he exhaled in turn represented his questions or desires transubstantiated into a form acceptable to the spirits. As soon as he lit his pipe, the smoker would exhale in the four cardinal directions—north, south, east then west—in order to orientate his prayers towards their intended recipients."

> "Birds were the most common animals carved on Adena/ Hopewell pipe bowls because of their ability to travel through the air, which was conceived of as a separate world. Ducks and other waterfowl were particularly popular because they were able to travel through all of the worlds: air, water and land."[1]

Tobacco pipes have since become one of the most iconic symbols of tobacco smoking. An integral part of most native cultures of North America, pipes became the most popular form of tobacco smoking by the European colonists until cigarettes became the dominant way of smoking. Native Americans went to extraordinary lengths in their decoration of pipes, and the pipes themselves became as significant as the tobacco itself.

> "Pipes were used to seal oaths, to declare war, and to provide safe conduct. The Omaha Indians who inhabited most of Oklahoma had

a pair of war pipes and a pair of peace pipes. The former were plain, the latter highly ornamented with feathers and tufts, whose arrangement was charged with significance, and the peace pipe of any particular tribe was as easily recognizable to other tribes as was the banner or the coat of arms of a feudal lord ... the pipe often served as a pass or safe conduct for a messenger through hostile territory."[2]

COLUMBUS ARRIVES IN AMERICA AND TOBACCO ARRIVES IN EUROPE

The relationship between tobacco and the invading cultures of Europe has always been a mixed one. By the time the Europeans came into contact with Native Americans, tobacco was more widely cultivated in the New World than maize. After its discovery by Europeans in the Caribbean, tobacco spread around the world more quickly than any other plant in history. This may be due to the extraordinary addictiveness of nicotine and to tobacco's quickly becoming a favorite with sailors and mariners, who took it with them on their travels. The Spanish, however, took a long time to accept tobacco. Their attitude was conditioned by their feelings toward the people they conquered – "a godless heathen people, doing the devil's work." No one smoked in Europe at the time of Spain's conquest of Central America. It was an alien act. However, the Spanish colonizers did eventually adopt the habit, even though the Catholic Church remained resolutely against it. Other colonizers in North America did not have the same antagonistic relationship to tobacco or the people who smoked it as did the Spanish and the Catholic Church, and tobacco began to be used by the first settlers soon after their arrival. From there it soon spread to Europe.

Tobacco was first brought to Europe by a Franciscan friar, Andre Thevet. Its active substance, "nicotine," however, was named after the Frenchman, Jean Nicot, who introduced Nicotiana rustica to Europe some 10 years later. Sir Walter Raleigh, the English sailor and adventurer, acquired the smoking habit while in Virginia and made it somewhat fashionable in England. However, when King James I of England came to the throne, he wrote diatribes against tobacco, doing his best to curb its use, yet fueling the public's disdain toward him in the process. Nevertheless, and in spite of high taxes, smoking spread throughout Europe. Raleigh, for his troubles, was beheaded by the king in 1618, and had his pipe in his mouth when the axe fell. On his pipe-case was the following inscription – "It was my companion in that most wretched time." During the 17th century, possession of tobacco was also a capital offence in Russia. Tobacco use was prohibited in many parts of Germany – punishable by torture, beheading, hanging, quartering or crushing. All the empires and nation states of Europe went through a love/hate relationship with tobacco. In general the Church disliked it, though many in the clergy who went to the New World to bring Christianity to the "heathens" developed snuff habits, a more acceptable way of imbibing tobacco, and its use in the New World spread from the clergy to their congregations. Governments in Europe often attempted to curtail indulgence in tobacco, depending on the whims and fancies of the current kings or rulers. However, over time, tobacco's taxation possibilities became too strong to resist, and many countries developed state monopolies, limiting domestic production, and controlling the supply, importation and distribution of tobacco.

Despite its early reluctance to embrace tobacco, Spain eventually took it on with gusto, building a huge cigar making factory in Seville at the beginning of the 19th century and employing young women because of their dexterity with their hands. Huge numbers of young women worked in this sweltering factory, often half naked because of the heat. As Gately puts it:

> "Seville is the birthplace of tobacco's association with sex in the old world. It had given Europe cigars, and many of the romantic associations attached to their consumption. Cigars were for bandeleros, for dashing cavalry officers, and they were prepared for these heroes lips by beautiful, semi-naked Andalusians, who also smoked."

Many Frenchman became enamored by the combination of cigars, women and Seville, giving inspiration to Prosper Merimee to write Carmen.

"The tale of a gypsy temptress who breaks hearts and steals watches."[3]

This is long after Pizarro destroyed the Inca civilization, reducing the population of Peru from 9 million in 1532 to 1.5 million by 1570. The irony of the conqueror's adoption of the habits of the vanquished is stated well by Gately:

> "When one civilization absorbs another via conquest, it sometimes adopts its victims' culture to the extent that is later hard to distinguish the victor from the vanquished. In such circumstances the vanquished entity may be said to have triumphed – through the perpetuation of its gods, its art, or its pleasures. The Aztecs and the Incas may have been destroyed by the Spaniards but their tobacco habits have been adopted since by the entire world. If an Aztec and a Roman were transported to the twenty-first century the Aztec might be the less mystified. He would know why people were smoking."[4]

Tobacco is only one of many addictive substances that was adopted by the colonizers. Coffee, tea, marijuana, opium and cocaine all came to western societies as a result of conquest and colonization of other cultures and it could be said that, in modern cultures, many of the descendents of the colonizers are now enslaved to these substances as a result of their ancestors' enslavement and mistreatment of other human beings.

When Jean Nicot brought tobacco to France, he attempted to justify its worth by pointing out its medicinal properties. The plants had previously been used in Europe for ornamental purposes, and grown in Royal Gardens but Nicot had heard of its possible effectiveness in treating cancer and had treated a man with a tumor, using an ointment made from tobacco leaves, which appeared to have affected a total cure. Nicot then sent some plants and seeds to the Queen of France, Catherine de'Medici, who was fascinated by such things as alchemy and magic. After she adopted the habit of taking tobacco as snuff, the practice spread throughout the fashionable circles in France. News of its use spread throughout Europe, the Pope even ordering that seeds be sown in the gardens of the Vatican. Tobacco's use as a cure-all spread throughout Europe while its use for pleasure also grew, and although at first domestic supply was sufficient tobacco began to be imported by France, initially from Cuba. Each country adopted its use in different ways, according somewhat to the temperament of the country at the time. To quote Gately:

> "A country's reaction to the introduction of tobacco was highly revealing of its national character. The French used it to ward off illness and preserve beauty; in the Italian states, it was entrusted to the care of priests and administered in their advice; in the German principalities it was examined in accordance with the best current scientific principles and declared a *violent herb;* in Switzerland it was tested first on a dog before being recommended for human consumption. One European country, however, focused on an entirely different justification for tobacco use: pleasure."[5]

The England of the Elizabethan age was full of swashbuckling bravado, with characters such as Sir Walter Raleigh, Sir Francis Drake and the English Navy often attacking Spanish galleons and heading off with their bounty. The English, having also been through the Reformation did not have such "Catholic" ideas regarding natives' use of tobacco and other substances and were therefore more willing to adopt those habits than their more conservative neighbors and enemies were. The Germans remained ambivalent toward tobacco and took a long time to widely accept its use, but other Protestant cultures such as the Dutch did very well with tobacco, as it aided their own imperial ventures. To this day they have maintained an intimate loyalty to tobacco, depending more on the roll-your-own variety than the machine-made cigarette.

The English adopted the pipe as their favored mode of inhalation (copying the native Americans they had met in the New World, who had perfected the practice of pipe-smoking for hundreds of years) in contrast to the cigar that the Spanish had seen used by the Incas and Aztecs of South and Central America. As Raleigh and others spread the news of tobacco amongst the high society of England, including Queen Elizabeth I, a smoking pipe became an accoutrement of respectable gentlemen, who traveled with an assortment of pipes, knives, tobacco and other "essentials"—often requiring a personal servant to carry them. Christopher Marlowe, author of *Dr. Faustus,* may have had an affinity for tobacco and is said to have made the statement, "All they that love not boys and tobacco are fools", (although it should be noted that his alleged "love" for boys has been disputed, and the quotation is thought by some historians to have been the work of his enemies who hoped to put his character in a dubious light.) Ben Jonson mentioned tobacco in his work, calling it an essential part of a man's life. Shakespeare, however, did not refer to smoking into his repertoire, leaving the question unanswered as to his fealty to the weed.

Despite its popularity tobacco was very expensive, and England, having no direct supply of it, had to rely on trade, piracy and smuggling. In many parts of Europe, it became a form of cash – one of the many times tobacco has served that purpose. The cultivation of home-grown tobacco helped alleviate the shortage but even high prices did not discourage people from eagerly buying tobacco from all sources, leading to shortages and the adulteration of tobacco, often by apothecaries, who sought to dominate its use as a medicine. This brought about the first public anti-smoking appeal by a Christian sect known as the Puritans who equated tobacco-use with devil worship. This first stab of puritanical rejection at the impulse for addiction was the beginning of an intermittent yet forceful struggle against tobacco and other 'sinful' substances, a sentiment that reached new heights in the Prohibition movement against alcohol in the United States in the 1920's.

Once tobacco took root in Europe it quickly spread to most parts of the globe that the Europeans had contact with, especially Africa. The Portuguese introduced it to the tribes they were in contact with in coastal trading ports, and it quickly spread into the interior of Africa where it was taken by both men and women. Often pipes were used, huge in size, holding pounds of tobacco, and tobacco became an essential part of their culture. Many Africans were already familiar with the practice of smoking – not tobacco, but cannabis or dagga. This helped the integration of tobacco into the rituals of their society.

King James I, who first publicly wrote of the evils of tobacco, also had an interest in the persecution of witches and used similar language in both cases—the forces of darkness and the devil being clearly at work. However few of his subjects agreed when it came to tobacco. Using tactics similar to those of many governments today, when he couldn't ban it, he decided to tax it – raising the duty on tobacco by 4000 per cent. A shortage of tobacco to tax, a peace treaty with Spain and a large navy in waiting gave England an incentive to send people to colonize the New World and establish permanent colonies. However, the first few that tried failed miserably. Finally, in 1612, John Rolfe managed to plant and produce tobacco that could be imported to England. This gave added financial impetus for the colonies to survive and attract new people, directly leading to slavery to cater for the labor needs to grow and harvest tobacco for the English, the local natives proving "unreliable" for such hard and unrewarding work.

TOBACCO AND SLAVERY

At the time of the first American settlement in the Virginia colony, Native Americans had long cultivated and used tobacco, chiefly the N. rustica species. The English settlers at Jamestown learned about tobacco from native chiefs Powhatan and Pehancanough. Members of their tribes introduced the English settlers to smoking and growing Nicotiana rustica, but the colonists who liked its stimulant properties were less fond of its harshness and psychoactive nature. In 1612, the year before he married Pocahontas (Powhatan's daughter), John Rolfe managed to obtain and bring to Virginia some seeds of Nicotiana tabacum, a much milder-smoking form. It is believed that Rolfe acquired his seeds from the Spanish or Portuguese in the Caribbean, since all of the tobacco grown by the Indians in eastern North America was Nicotiana rustica. Nicotiana tabacum was mild in other ways as well, as it did not contain harmaline, the psychoactive alkaloid, and this was the variety of tobacco plant that farmers elected to grow. At this time, tobacco use was rapidly expanding in Europe. American colonists saw that tobacco could be an extremely profitable cash crop for trading with the Old World and set out to commercialize its production.

The colonists' energetic focus on tobacco's potential as a cash crop subverted both traditional ways of growing it and the relationship between tobacco and its human users. In Native American belief, tobacco was a gift of the gods to humanity, and the plant itself a sacred being. Its use by humans was a shared interaction between the human and tobacco spirits; its life and habitat had to be respected. The Algonquins, the major tribe in Virginia and the Carolinas, grew tobacco by methods that avoided tilling, irrigation, clearing of forestland, or killing of the sacred plant. Seeds were planted in natural clearings and left unfertilized, although the areas around the growing plants were carefully weeded. The land was selected for adequate rainfall or tributary drainage rather than provided with water from artificial sources. The plant itself, an annual which matures in one year and dies naturally in late autumn, was allowed to fulfill this cycle while the lowest leaves ripened and were collected periodically for regular drying and smoking, carefully wrapped in bracken fronds to prevent damage, and cured, often in the same sweathouses as were used for spiritual cleansing. Algonquin culture also divided duties by gender, so while men conducted warfare and hunting, women were the chief farmers, the nurture of growing things being regarded as an expression of the female spirit. Such agriculture methods did not require a great amount of labor.

But the colonists did not become attuned to this reciprocal natural relationship with tobacco. To them, tobacco occupied a subservient role similar to that of cattle, whose natural cycle had to be subordinated to the financial needs of humans. When John Rolfe's importation of Nicotiana tabacum seeds gave colonists the docile smoke they wanted, they began to demand crop maximization to garner European trading profits. Huge swathes of virginal forest were razed to provide tobacco plantations, and plans to irrigate the dry areas of this land were set in place. The growth of young tobacco plants was artificially sped up by fertilization with the waste products of farm animals. In the late summer, while the plants were still living, they would be cut down en masse and tossed on heaps to be cured, bundled, transported, and shipped to Europe. All of this extra horticultural and shipping work demanded labor-intensive methods in a region with sparse human settlements, and led directly to attempts by the colonists to harness the Native Americans to perform the labor.

Such attempts were abortive. By no means would the Algonquins submit to such enforced labor, which violated both the sacred role of the tobacco plant and the relationship of mutual help between Indians and English settlers, as well as violating the Algonquins' view of the types of work appropriate to men or to women. As soon as English tobacco farmers stopped watching them, their Indian "laborers" would escape, never to be seen again. Colonial Virginia planters discovered that they needed many reliably permanent workers as an inexpensive source of labor to help grow tobacco and get it ready to be shipped to England. At first they used indentured servants, imported from England, but as plantation agriculture spread up the Potomac River, the demand for field workers exceeded the supply of people in the colonies and England who were willing to do such work. In 1619 (only 7 years after the first planting of Nicotiana tabacum) a Dutch ship brought the first African captives to Virginia.

Even these first Africans imported to work in Virginia tobacco fields were commonly given indentured status and allowed eventually to purchase their own freedom. They were not automatically slaves. Some held property, married, and raised families outside the institution of slavery. However, in the 1660's, the end of England's civil war, which was making emigration less attractive, reduced the supply of indentured servants from England to well below the number of laborers needed in Virginia. To meet the practical demand, the government of the colony (not the officials in London) established the legal framework for perpetual servitude based on color.

By the end of the 1660's, the Virginia colony had effectively revised its laws to establish that blacks could be kept in slavery permanently, generation after generation. At the same time, an influx of slaves was spurred by a drop in the value of sugar grown on Caribbean islands, causing the planters there to sell their slave "property" to the tobacco farmers in Virginia. As a result, as tobacco ascended to become the most profitable agricultural product in the Virginia colony, so did slavery ascend to become the dominant source of workers for its production.

Untold thousands of Africans were brought over on crowded ships against their will, to provide the manual labor for Virginia's tobacco industry. Most of these slaves were not imported from Africa but from the Caribbean, where the slavery model of labor production had long been applied to sugar fields. Having whipped to death the Native Americans originally enslaved to work the sugar, the Spanish and French settlers held the general belief that Africans were naturally more capable of hard labor in the tropical Caribbean climate than were the Indians. Although Virginia did not have a tropical climate, the shift of Caribbean slaves to its plantations introduced the slavery model of agricultural production to its shores. It is interesting to note that John Rolfe had originally imported his first Nicotiana tabacum seeds to Virginia from the Caribbean, so it seems that enslaved human beings and the "tamed" tobacco species were brought to Virginia from the same geographical region.

Virginia tobacco planters would begin cultivating their tobacco crop in late December or early January. The entire season of planting and harvesting tobacco lasted into August and September, when the tobacco plants were finally cut, dried, and packed in hogsheads (large barrels or casks) to be shipped to England. The hogsheads were then carried by wagon or boat to inspection sites such as the one in Fredericksburg, Virginia, or were even rolled by hand. Slaves planted and harvested the tobacco crop, built the shipping barrels, delivered the harvested and cured tobacco to the inspection warehouses, and loaded and unloaded the ships preparing for sail to England, essentially performing all of the labor, while the English, owners of both crop and laborers, received the profit.

According to the colonial concept of tobacco growing, the slaves who provided the labor were not fellow humans, but were, instead, regarded by their owners as "capital investment". They were owned by the planters, bought and sold by the planters, and did not give "birth to children" but rather "produced more slaves" who were also considered a cash crop to be bought and sold. Furthermore, the tobacco they toiled to grow became the economic measure of the slaves' living worth. There were no banks in colonial Virginia and no American coinage, although English currency could be used. Barter rather than actual money was commonly employed for trade and exchange. Colonial Virginians could buy goods from merchants and shopkeepers on credit and pay their debts when their crops were harvested and sold. Tobacco became a highly-bartered item that was used as money, being grown and then sold in England for profits that would be used to buy more tools of tobacco production, such as seed, land, and slaves. Inspectors at public warehouses where tobacco was sold also issued tobacco certificates for transacting business. Some of the most important business was the importing of slaves for further plantation work, and slaves themselves were commonly bought and sold, with tobacco being used as the medium of exchange. Thus, tobacco and the Africans who had been forced to work to produce it had both rapidly come to be seen as despiritualized factors of wealth production for their owners.

A 'triangular trade' was established during the next century between Africa, the east coast shipping ports in America, and Bristol, England. Bristol slaving ships would set out for Africa with items such as cloth and mirrors to be traded with local African chiefs for humans to be used as slaves. The ships then set out for America with their human cargo to be sold and traded in the slave markets of Virginia and the Carolinas. On the last leg, back to Bristol, the slave ships would carry crops such as cotton, tobacco and rice, slave-grown, to be traded for English currency so that the triangle would be completed and continued through further cycles.

Tobacco production thrived in the American South during the next two hundred years, supported by the slave economy that made handsome profits for plantation owners. However, although the slave-driven tobacco economy was amenable to profits, American abolitionists spoke out strongly against it. William Lloyd Garrison, the New York newspaper editor, founder of the New England Anti-Slavery Society, and a chief figure in both the American Abolition movement and the Abstinence movement, decried tobacco as the literal cause of slavery in the South. In his paper, The Liberator (1830-65), he proclaimed tobacco to be slavery's progenitor. Garrison pointed out that the culture of tobacco had brought slavery to America, and that seven out of ten slaves in the United States were employed in its production. Garrison observed also that "tobacco produces a fierce enslavement of those who use it" and – linking the slavery it can produce to the slavery used in its production – tried in vain to dissuade freemen from buying slave-produced tobacco. Tobacco abstinence was an intrinsic part of the temperance movement, which worked to persuade people to forego alcohol and other addictive substances. Tobacco fed slavery and slavery fed tobacco, in Garrison's system, and only the rigid ethical refusal to buy or use it could interrupt the vicious economic cycle.

President Lincoln credited Garrison's writings with being the tool which originally turned his mind to the injustices of slavery. Its economic underpinnings were interrupted by the American Civil War, which was preceded by Lincoln's tactical declaration of the manumission of the slaves in all states. Although this strategic move ended the official American slave economy, it has not ended the enduring association between slavery and tobacco.

In India, young children have been enslaved into bonded servitude for many generations, cigarette production being one of the largest economies using this labor. This type of slavery passes through generations, the debt of the father being carried on by the son. Only in recent years has this situation been addressed by both the Indian government and western countries. In 1976, the Indian government outlawed bonded servitude throughout the country, but in more remote areas it is still practiced, some observers estimating that at least 10 million people are still in bonded labor. It is now illegal to import products into the United States that are produced by bonded labor.

Among the different species of tobacco, the one used most by Native Americans, Nicotiana rustica, imposes its own demands of mental and spiritual interaction on the user. It is N. rustica that was grown by

Native Americans in a harmonious interrelationship of humans, plant, and environment, N. rustica that repelled the European taste for a mild smoke, which could be a pastime rather than a spiritual exercise, and N. rustica that essentially "resisted" compliance with the European desire for large-scale profiteering. The domesticated version, N. tabacum, humbly met European wishes, but also demanded slave labor, as well as chemically enslaving its users.

This suggests a split in the nature of tobacco itself, similar to the split observed within certain groups of animals, such as the dog and wolf, both from the genus Canis, part of which has become domesticated and part of which has resisted domestication, remaining free and wild. Nicotiana rustica is the original American form of tobacco, allied with Native Americans and used by them to enhance their spiritual practice (although there is ample evidence of it also being abused.) It is raised by traditional methods and smoked today by Indian tribes as part of their sacred heritage. In contrast, Nicotiana tabacum has adapted itself to human demands as a generic crop that can be bought, sold, traded, and used in a system that holds little concern for the spiritual aspects of human life, or the potential health dangers of its products – choosing, instead, a narrow focus on making profits. Such a division symbolically identifies N. tabacum with the European settlers who overran the American continent, as well as with their human, mostly African, slaves. This creates a loop between buyer, user, and substance: the user is compelled to buy more to satisfy his craving, and the grower is compelled to grow more in order to remain financially viable. N. rustica, on the other hand, seems to maintain its identification with wild, pre-colonial America and with the Native American tribes who themselves used and grew it. This split suggests a polar tension in the nature of the Nicotiana genus along the axis of freedom and slavery, with N. tabacum as the emblem of slavery and N. rustica as the emblem of resistance against it.

THE ACCEPTANCE OF TOBACCO IN EUROPEAN SOCIETY.

It took some time for tobacco to be truly accepted in European countries, most going through a number of phases during which it was banned—at times under the threat of death—or was highly controlled and taxed upon. James I of England relentlessly tried to ban it, and the ban continued under his son, King Charles I, only to be eased after the onset of the English Civil War. Spain tried to control tobacco by regulating where it could be grown and where it could not. In some places the sale of tobacco or tobacco seeds was punishable by death. Seville became the only place where tobacco importing was allowed, which eventually led to the building of a huge cigar factory inhabited by half-naked young Spanish women. The local priests took a distinct liking to "sniffing" tobacco, copying their colleagues in the new world, until the Pope threatened them with excommunication. Whatever the official ideas about tobacco were, governments soon realized the taxable potential of tobacco and therefore sought various levels of control and state monopoly over the supply and distribution of the weed. Much of this tax went to fund the armies of Europe, which – from the 1620's to the 1640's – were engaged in the Thirty-Years War. The Protestant Dutch, perhaps the most liberal and progressive society in Europe at the time, took up smoking with enthusiasm, advocating its use for every imaginable ill, including the plague, and even encouraging small children to take up the habit. "A Dutchman without a pipe is a national impossibility. If a Dutchman were deprived of his pipe and tobacco, he would not even enter paradise with a glad heart."[6] The Dutch, in a true expression of the Protestant work ethic, ensured their supply of tobacco mainly by trading or by plunder, enjoying the fruits of Spanish galleons and, in the process, clearing the waters of the Caribbean of the Spanish Navy. Most importantly they brought slaves to the Americas in large numbers. These slaves were bought with tobacco.

In Russia and Turkey, however, the people were prohibited from using tobacco while in Persia, merchants caught selling tobacco were executed by having molten lead poured down their throats!

In the Ottoman Empire, Murad IV, also known as Murad the Cruel, who ruled between 1623 and 1640, hated smoking and would dress in disguise, asking people for a smoke and then beheading anybody who obliged. In a 14-year period, he apparently put to death 25,000 suspected smokers. A change of ruler in the Ottoman Empire brought a more sympathetic official attitude regarding tobacco, and the Ottomans adopted the Persian water pipe as their means of smoking. The Church in the German state of Saxony in 1653 decided that tobacco was of evil intent, stating: "it is both godless and unseemly that the mouth of man, which is the means of entrance and exit of the immortal soul, that mouth which is intended to breathe in the fresh air and to utter the praises of the most high, should be defiled by the indrawing and expelling of tobacco smoke."

For the European countries that had specific interests in the economic possibilities of international trade, tobacco became the essential medium of exchange. In other words, it was money itself. This is extraordinary for a substance that had no seemingly essential function apart from enjoyment and ritual. One couldn't eat it, it wasn't intrinsically rare, yet it acted to stimulate extraordinary social and economic exchange throughout the known world. In 1652, the Dutch purchased the entire peninsula of the Cape of Good Hope for a "certain quantity of tobacco and brandy."[7]

For the English, tobacco became the great democratizer. Although smoking and snuff were eventually adopted as part of the formal rituals of the ruling class, tobacco was enjoyed by all the subjects of King and Queen, apart from those who couldn't afford it. It became an essential tool in the quest for learning, assuming a role similar to its role among the Aztecs' that of meditation, feeding the human spirit, not the body. Isaac Newton smoked his whole life, apparently incessantly. "The weed was so integral to his identity that he was once observed in a fit of mental abstraction, using the finger of the lady he was courting as a tobacco stopper, as he sat and smoked in silence beside her." It was an inspiration to the poets, Robert Herrick and John Milton, Herrick celebrating tobacco in his poetry:

It is all spirit, not to force belief,
It is the life of air, the air of life.

Here, all alone, I by myself have took,
An emblem of myself, a Pipe of Smoke.
For, I am but a little piece of clay
Filled with smoke that quickly fumes away.[8]

"Smoking became a metaphor for mutability – the evanescence of pleasure, indeed, of existence itself – and was a favorite subject of meditations upon transience."[9]

Daniel Defoe, in his story of Robinson Crusoe, ensured his castaway discovered a lot of tobacco, which Crusoe then smokes in a home made clay pipe, allaying his isolation and giving him the necessary inspiration to survive and prosper in his surroundings.

The Scots became the great tobacco merchants by the end of the 17th century, and when Scotland and England became one country, many tobacco merchants made a fortune. The connection between the trading posts and colonies of the New World and the port of Glasgow was strong, with slaves and tobacco constantly changing hands. Tobacco was still the main lifeline between the new and old worlds, and the richest man in Virginia—indeed, in all the British colonies -was a tobacco farmer, Robert "King" Carter, who owned over 300,000 acres of land and 390 slaves of working age.

Tobacco became North America's principal export by value throughout the eighteenth century, representing nearly half of total exports in 1750.

THE AGE OF ENLIGHTENMENT

As the Eighteenth century unfolded and the influences of the Age of Enlightenment rippled through European society, the use of tobacco continued to evolve, mainly in the form in which it was taken. The proclivity of the English and Dutch for using pipes and the preference for "ceegars" of the Spanish were now often being replaced by a penchant for snuff, especially by the clergy and the ruling class. It became, as much as anything a fashion statement, but many of the great thinkers of the age were devoted smokers and sniffers. The French had been dedicated snuff-takers since Jean Nicot introduced Nicotiana rustica, which was brought into the theater by Moliere in 1665, when a character in the play proclaims, holding snuff box in hand: "Whatever Aristotle and all the philosophy might say, there is nothing to equal tobacco; it is the passion of honest people, and he who lives without tobacco is not worthy of living. Not only does it rejuvenate and purge the human brain, but it also instructs the soul on virtue and teaches one to become an honest man."

The British also adopted snuff with gusto, conveniently incorporating it into the rituals and measures of class status, a person's caliber being measured by the shape and quality of his snuff box. Smokers began to be seen as more lower class, the committed snifter much superior, as his habit was more rarefied than brutish smoking. Problems with adulteration of both snuff and tobacco led to further government involvement and taxation, which then led to riots in the streets as the government attempted to define tobacco as a luxury, not a necessity – an issue continually debated and influenced by other political and social dynamics. Adam Smith, the father of modern economics chimed in on the subject:

> "It is the highest impertinence and presumption, therefore in kings and ministers, to pretend to watch over the economy of private people, and to restrain their expense, either by sumptuary laws, or by prohibiting the importation of foreign luxuries. They are themselves always, and without exception, the greatest spendthrifts in society. Let them look well after their own expense, and they may safely trust private people with theirs. If their own extravagance does not ruin the state, that of their subjects never will."[10]

Once tobacco had become firmly established in Britain and the rest of Europe, the newly inspired imperial nations exported it to those parts of the world that hadn't enjoyed the privilege of indulging themselves with smoking. However, when the British came across the Aboriginals of Australia, they found a people who already partook of their own variety of tobacco. For a nomadic people who had not established any means of plant cultivation, tobacco was an exception, and they would stay in one area until they could harvest their crop. The Aboriginals mainly chewed tobacco but, similar to the way in which the British viewed tobacco, it conferred a certain status within Aboriginal community and was used as a means of exchange. However, not long after the first convicts and other white settlers came to Australia, bringing their own tobacco habits with them—

along with smallpox and other diseases from Europe—the cultural and spiritual relationship with tobacco was reduced to an indulgence.

The economic impact of tobacco had its most significant influence through the impetus it gave to the American War of Independence, the colonists rebelling against the intention of Mother England to levy more tobacco taxes. Jefferson was a tobacco farmer, as was Washington, and even though the levy being imposed in the Colonies was much less than the one imposed on British subjects at home, it fueled a simmering republican movement and consequently the Revolutionary War. When the thirteen colonies signed the Declaration of Independence, tobacco was never far from their minds, as most were involved in the tobacco trade. It was also in the minds and noses of most English people, including that of the mentally unstable King George III and his wife, Queen Charlotte. England's vanity led to a cavalier attitude toward its wayward colonists in the New World, not to mention bemusement at the colonists' fascination with notions of freedom and liberty, combined with their devotion to slavery. The War of Independence led to a huge increase in the price of tobacco in England, which led to the cultivation of a home-grown form ruthlessly suppressed by the King's army who was determined to control the supply, and of course its taxation. The Scots had stockpiled their supplies in Glasgow and again made a hefty profit from the situation.

Tobacco was also the form of payment rendered to the French by Benjamin Franklin for assisting the Colonists in their fight against the British. The French King, having no particular affinity with the Colonists' notions of republicanism, was tempted by the amount of tobacco offered, along with the enjoyment of getting one back on the English. After the war, and to pay for the ongoing expenses of the French court, the French king tried to impose punitive taxes on a number of items - including, of course, tobacco. Soon after, the French had their own revolution, and the "noble" habit of snuffing tobacco was quickly dropped in favor of smoking, in case some guillotine-happy person took exception. Again, tobacco was never far removed from the quest for liberation as well as the tyranny of oppression.

It didn't take long for tobacco to be seen as a form of revenue for the new French Republic, but it wasn't until Napoleon held the reins that tobacco taxation really took hold, born from a necessity to fund the constant state of war that Napoleon seemed to enjoy. As Europe fell into a siege of war, the demand for tobacco increased dramatically, being spread by the very soldiers who were doing their duty by Napoleon. Also, as Napoleon was a committed sniffer, the art of snuff-taking came back to the fore. While Napoleon was heading for his Waterloo, smoking tobacco became the more popular way of imbibing, and the Spanish habit of cigar smoking becoming the most common form. Smoking was enjoyed by all strata of society, whereas sniffing was always a more exclusive way of using tobacco.

Another common association of tobacco with banditry and smuggling rose again in the mountains of Spain, especially in Andalusia, where more than 100 years later Ernest Hemingway would smoke cigars while watching bullfighting. Andalusia has always been bandit country, and even in the midst of Franco's Fascist regime, outlaw groups continued to hold out. Like the infamous pirates 200 years before, who smoked like fiends, the bandeleros smoked cigars, being forever stamped with the connection to machismo, (calling to mind the image of Fidel Castro smoking his Havana while Kennedy and Co decide whether to drop the bomb on Cuba!)

Although the habits of snuffing and smoking remained very popular well into the 19th century in England, being advanced by the new Romantic movement and writers such as Wordsworth, Coleridge, and Lord Byron, smoking was still not seen as something to do in public arenas—a far cry from the smoky pubs found in 20th century England. Therefore, places to smoke and clothes to smoke in became part of the smoking ritual, also providing a convenient excuse to separate the men from the women! The increase in the smoking of cigars led to the creation of smoking shops, or tobacconists, and also specific places reserved for smoking, similar to the places in Turkey used for smoking hookahs. Pipe smoking came back into fashion in England, suited more for the mature and wise of society than the young and rakish. Thackeray said, "The pipe draws wisdom from the lips of the philosopher, and shuts up the mouth of the foolish; it generates a style of conversation, contemplative, thoughtful, benevolent and unaffected."

The fascination with pipes was still much stronger in the United States where the elaborate rituals, symbols, and practical significance of pipe smoking were such an significant part of indigenous culture. However, the smoking of cigars did spread throughout the country in the 19th Century, as did the habit of chewing tobacco, which perhaps as much as smoking tobacco, had distinct antisocial consequences. Charles Dickens, when visiting America, was appalled by the habit of chewing tobacco. He wrote about it extensively and, although a cigar smoker himself, it apparently tempered his republican sympathies.

The cigarette first began to appear in Spain, and then was taken to France where it got its name. The Carmen-like women, smoking tobacco wrapped in paper, oozing sultry sensuality, gave birth to the connection of smoking with sexuality – and, in particular, female sexuality. This connection, along with the symbolic statement of liberation that smoking gave to women, has been exploited ever since, as in the movies of the early Hollywood years when strong independent women like Lauren Bacall smoked luxuriantly, even taking the cigarette from the mouth of the suave Humphrey Bogart. The cause of the cigarette was greatly aided by the development of a lighter-colored tobacco leaf, which allowed inhalation of the smoke deep into the lungs without overwhelming the smoker. The spread of the cigarette was also influenced by its method of production, as machines were now able to make them in vast numbers. However, it still took time for cigarette smoking to take over as the world's favorite form of enjoying tobacco.

THE VICTORIAN ERA AND THE INDUSTRIAL REVOLUTION

In Victorian England, cigars and pipes remained immensely popular, tobacco companies emphasizing the individual nature of the smoker in contrast to the 20th century attitude of maximizing the consumption by consumers. Many of the great thinkers of that time were dedicated smokers. Oscar Wilde loved his cigarettes, Karl Marx puffed away on cigars and Charles Darwin both smoked and snuffed. Prince Albert liked his cigars though his wife required him to have his own smoking room. As the 19th century progressed and England's empire reaped rewards, a new breed of person developed - the middle class - and tobacco shared in this development. "Smoking gave a clarity to the class system through which a smoker could proceed as his wealth increased. How the habit was prosecuted defined the man. The middle class found its totem in the pipe. It was the perfect device for expressing both individuality and respectability."[11] However, Victorian morals could not quite give in to too much pleasure and a separation of men and women occurred during the smoking ritual. The smoking of tobacco in pipes came to often symbolize the period of a young man's life as he built his career in preparation for marriage, and, once married, was expected to give up smoking, as if the freedom that smoking represented was inconsistent with the responsibilities of middle class Victorian life. This predicament was written about in J.M. Barrie's book *My Lady Nicotine.* It seemed a strange burden to bear, the weight of Victorian morality bearing down upon the new and hardworking middle classes – whereas, in both the upper and lower levels of the social strata, such constraints were not considered. But as tobacco was a fearful temptress, men could not divest themselves of such a mistress and after dinner, the women were often sent from the room, leaving the men with their pipes and cigars. Taking tobacco as an enema became another way to use the weed for Victorians, who developed an intense concern for the regularity of their bowels. The English, being enthusiastic writers, wove tobacco into their stories, with characters such as Sherlock Holmes smoking pipes, cigars and cigarettes to aid his sleuthing in the foggy streets of London.

The English, while pursuing their imperial agenda took tobacco with them, fulfilling the plants' natural inclination toward communications between "different worlds". In India, tobacco was quickly adopted, mostly being smoked and chewed, and India became a huge producer of tobacco, harvesting the equivalent of 4/5ths of the total American harvest, the world's biggest producer. In Africa, the British came across a people already firmly entrenched in their relationship with tobacco, but again tobacco accompanied them in their journeys into the heart of the continent. Most of the British in the 19th century were still established pipe and cigar smokers as the cigarette had not taken hold yet. The fact that cigarettes were still identified with the French did not encourage their use—everything French being seen as suspect, effeminate and worse. Oscar Wilde was one of the notable exceptions to this, chain-smoking cigarettes, but as he was notably gay, it only confirmed the British prejudice against all things French. Many Americans held a similar opinion to the cigarette, the New York Times stating "The decadence of Spain began when the Spaniards adopted cigarettes and if this pernicious practice obtains among adult Americans the ruin of the Republic is close at hand."[12]

However, the convenience of cigarettes, along with the invention of the friction match in England, led to the steady increase in cigarette smoking, and it wasn't long before the manufacturers began to actively market cigarettes, creating advertising campaigns that focused on a brand name and identification for the cigarette – a new phenomenon in the use of tobacco. Before, the individuality of the smoker was the important thing, but now the brand of tobacco was the key, with different brands for different strata of society. In both the United States and England, cigarettes were made by machines by the 1870's, allowing huge numbers to be produced. Cigarettes also suited the times, with an increasing urban population needing the convenience of a "quick smoke", no longer having the time to luxuriantly enjoy a cigar or pipe. Cigarettes therefore democratized smoking in a radical way, opening up the habit for more and more people and allowing it to become accepted as part of daily activity, not as a separate, exclusive experience. Cigarette smoking seemed designed to be shared, as opposed to the solitary spirit of the pipe and the individualism of the cigar.

The popularity of cigarettes also had to do with the milder form of tobacco used, allowing people to take up smoking without dealing with the initial trauma of taking into the body the dark, strong smoke from cigar and pipe tobacco. The method of curing tobacco used in cigarettes allowed the smoke to be inhaled into the lungs where the nicotine could be absorbed easily into the body, in contrast to the cigar and pipe where the smoke is taken in through the mucous membranes of the mouth and throat. Drawing smoke into the lungs seemed to invoke a peculiar pleasure, an experience where an unnatural and even painful act can evoke a pleasurable response. "Smokers describe the sensation of inhaling as a tactile delight. The collision of smoke with lungs is an exquisite torture, and the practice of inhaling is as addictive as tobacco itself.[13]

Even though the tobacco used in cigarettes was milder than that which was used in cigars and pipes, they were still much stronger than most that are smoked today, and generally did not have as many additives—so most smokers would not smoke more than 10 a day, in contrast to the 40 or 60 a day for some committed smokers of the late 20th century. Even at the beginning of the 20th century, with cigarette manufacturing being highly mechanized, American smoking habits seemed to reach saturation point, leading major tobacco companies to look for new markets. The new American Tobacco Company, a trust created by the major tobacco companies to control the supply of tobacco, attempted to muscle in on the British smoking scene, which had also established powerful companies such as Imperial Tobacco (a suitable name at the pinnacle of Victoria's reign, when Britain still ruled the waves). The American invasion faltered when they were neither able to persuade the British public to switch allegiances nor take over the British companies. The result of this was a truce—the two countries leaving each other's markets to themselves—and a new, jointly owned company was created, named British American Tobacco, whose goal was to exploit the tobacco potential in the rest of the world (an early taste of the dynamics of global interests and the "special relationship" between the two countries).

After the death of Queen Victoria, the enthusiasm for smoking in England was enhanced by the ascendence to the throne of Edward VII, who announced to friends in Buckingham Palace, 'Gentlemen, you may smoke.' Smoking had by then infiltrated all parts of modern society; most people smoked, including people of influence. Smoking in all its forms was to be found in major pieces of cultural expression in art and literature, and then to be cemented some years later in the movies of Hollywood. However, smoking did not have a free ride:

The English government passed a law allowing only people above the age of 16, and the temperance movement in the United States also had an impact on tobacco use. However, the economic potential of cigarettes, for both the tobacco companies and the Government's tax burden, was far too tempting for much concern to be given to the physical and spiritual risks of smoking. Furthermore, no substantive scientific evidence about the harmful effects of tobacco existed at that time. Denying the existence of scientific evidence of tobacco's adverse effects continued to be a key strategy for tobacco companies for another 100 years, in spite of the accumulating evidence to the contrary.

CIGARETTES, WAR AND THE 20TH CENTURY

The developing debate regarding the health virtues and vices of tobacco was diminished in the face of the "Great War," which sucked Europe and also America into a cycle of human destruction as had never been seen before. In the midst of this horror, tobacco was a major refuge and solace to ease the emotional trauma of war and death. Cigarettes were an indispensable part of a soldier's rations, tobacco becoming a necessity, not a luxury. One of the notable writers of the time, Siegfried Sassoon, spoke about the significance of tobacco when he was on front lines:

> "I could hear the reloading click of rifle bolts on the lip of the crater above me as I crawled along with mud-clogged fingers. I knew that nothing in my previous experience of patrolling had ever been so grim as this, and I lay quite still for a bit, miserably wondering whether my number was up: then I remembered I was wearing my pre-war raincoat; I could feel the pipe and tobacco pouch in my pocket and somehow this made me feel less forlorn."[14]

A man facing death finds that having the company of tobacco helps him face the situation with greater equanimity. Perhaps this was because tobacco was familiar and could soothe the nerves, thus serving to humanize an otherwise inhuman situation. Cigarettes were shared, even amongst enemies—a statement of a shared predicament, a recognition of the fact that, in the moment of smoking together, the insanity of war is held at bay. This ritual, like the tobacco rituals of other cultures in other times, again reveals the role of tobacco as an intermediary—facilitating communication between peoples across space and time, between levels of consciousness. To quote from Gately:

> "Tobacco's spiritual importance to the men on the frontline is harder to define. In so many ways, a cigarette was a representation of their own existence—a short-lived, expendable item, transformed by fire into spirit and ashes. It was a symbol of mutability, like the blood-red poppies that sprouted every summer in no-man's land. It was also a token of security, however transitory. Cigarettes were smoked in minutes of rest, in periods of calm, and so were associated with such moments. The freedom to smoke a cigarette implied that the combatant had survived—for now."[15]

When the Americans joined the war in 1917, they brought their cigarettes with them. The generous rations for the American soldiers were appreciated by all the allied troops, and the names of the American brands such as Camel and Lucky Strike entered the lexicon of war language.

In the time of war the established order of things breaks down and, when put back together, is never quite the same again. During the war, women had taken on the reins of production, keeping the domestic economies going as the men trudged off to the trenches. This incidental emancipation from traditional roles gave women the opportunity to smoke—a statement of independence and financial solvency, as well as a way of relieving the traumas of war time. Soon after the war, women in Europe also got the vote and the previous taboos against women smoking carried much less weight. Tobacco companies increasingly looked to the potential market of women smokers and began to design brands to suit female sensibilities. Cigarettes' original female identity, beginning in the steamy factories of Seville and extending to the projection of effete Frenchmen and other "gay" types such as Oscar Wilde seemed to come full circle with women embracing the cigarette after World War One. Upper class women also saw the cigarette as a statement of freedom, liberating them from the social strictures of persistent Victorianism. Many of the returning soldiers were inevitably also addicted to cigarettes. Tobacco's original position as part of the rituals of middle and upper class life had changed after the war and now tobacco was regarded as a typical ingredient in a working man's design. The American tobacco companies were particularly keen to entice women to the fold and went to work creating brands that women would find attractive. Philip Morris created the "Marlboro" brand, named after the Duke of Marlborough, specifically designed for the discerning middle-class woman, quite different from the ubiquitous "Marlboro man" image of a later era. Claims that cigarettes had health benefits such as reducing people's desire to overeat, thus promoting weight-loss, also helped to stimulate demand. More and more women began to smoke, convinced that their figures were safer with cigarettes. This impetus faltered during the Great Depression, but even then, those who could afford to smoke still did, despite the fact that governments had raised taxes on tobacco, assuming this would deter people from smoking.

More than any other factor in the 20th century, apart from war, the advent of the film industry in Hollywood with the newly celebrated movie-star consolidated the prominent role of cigarettes in modern society. Smoking became a crucial element of characterization, the very identity of a film star being merged with his/her smoking habit. In the early days of cinema Hollywood faced the challenge of addressing sex in movie making, in a town and country where sexual morality exerted a significant influence. As a result of the inhibition of overt sexual expression, the art of smoking become an allegorical representation of sexual/sensual communication, further bonding the identity of the star to smoking. Whereas the film star mostly smoked cigarettes, people working behind the scenes often preferred cigars. When Eleanor Roosevelt herself was seen smoking a cigar, one would have expected tobacco's triumph of social acceptance to become final.

However, in Europe, one leader did not share in the people's enthusiasm for tobacco – Adolph Hitler. By the mid-1930's his disdain for smoking was public policy: smoking was banned in some public places and taxation on tobacco raised to extreme levels. Even so, until 1939, people smoked in increasing amounts in Germany, and tobacco was a significant tax earner in Germany's build-up to war. As war loomed, smoking fulfilled its soothing role and although Hitler still tried to restrict his soldiers' habits by limiting their cigarette rations, most soldiers had an ample supply to keep them going. Cigarettes were often given the same importance as medical supplies, being deemed a necessity for optimal upkeep of the soldier. Both during and after the war, the other major function of tobacco came to the fore, as a form of currency. Especially in Germany, cigarettes became an important means of exchange for a country debilitated by the war. The government attempted to impose a limit on domestic production, but much of the tobacco was being imported and smuggled in from the rest of Europe and the United States. The war had also fixed American and British brand names, such as Camel, Lucky Strike, Chesterfield and Pall Mall into the collective consciousness. This increased post-war cigarette smoking in many parts of the world. Tobacco became embedded in the establishment of peace, with America sending a gift of 210 million cigarettes to the German authorities, as part of the Marshall plan. Post-war Europe saw similar tectonic shifts in social consciousness. The age of rock 'n' roll further liberated people from traditional constraints, and the Hollywood images continued to flaunt the relationship between "man" and his cigarette, with Bogart and James Dean representing their respective generations.

The health consequences of tobacco use began to be seriously explored after World War Two instead of the supposed benefits of smoking being exploited and exaggerated for economic gain. The possible damage caused by tobacco smoking began to be more seriously questioned. One of the ways that tobacco companies addressed this was to put filters on cigarettes – something that many companies resisted like the plague (a disease that had justified the smoking of tobacco in a previous era). The facts that the filters were initially made from asbestos had repercussions for tobacco companies and their consumers that became more evident in the following decades.

As filters became widely used, it became more difficult for smokers to distinguish quality in tobacco, as much of the flavor they had once enjoyed was blocked. When tobacco companies realized this they began to put reconstituted sheet tobacco (RST) into cigarettes, including many parts of the tobacco plant that had previously been thrown away. It was apparent that, for the first time, the importance of image had usurped the position that once had been held by quality, and many kinds of cigarettes became almost indistinguishable.

As televisions began to appear in nearly every living room in the western world, tobacco companies saw another perfect medium to entice people to take up smoking. In the words of Gately:

> "In 1951, Philip Morris sponsored a new show called I Love Lucy. It was the top-rated show for four of its first six full seasons, during which its characters smoked a prodigious amount of cigarettes."[16]

Magazines also provided tobacco companies with a useful medium for advertising and encouraging the liberalization of social mores, as seen in the first publication of *Playboy* in 1953, where tobacco advertisements celebrated the connection between sex and smoking. One thing led to the next and the emerging image of the Marlboro Man took its place in the annals of smoking lore.

The British, watching their empire evaporate after such a long and exhausting war, continued to smoke like chimneys, dominating the charts in the sheer quantities consumed. In 1949, in England, 81% of men smoked and 39% of women. The ways they smoked and what they smoked, however, still reflected the embedded class structures of the country. The populace, depressed by the depleted state of post-war Britain, found some solace in the figure of James Bond – a dashing figure Sir Walter Raleigh would have been proud of. Bond's smoking habits were lavishly displayed while he fulfilled his duties to Her Majesty the Queen. Bond managed to perfectly entwine the dynamics of sexuality and smoking, facing perpetual danger with a calm that most non-smokers would find hard to understand. However, the weight of scientific evidence against tobacco forced its way onto the screen in the movie Thunderball, where Bond was told that his cigarette and alcohol habits were not doing him any good.

As the incidence of lung cancer increased, pressure on tobacco companies to admit the dangers of tobacco-smoking also grew. However, finding them legally responsible was another matter. The level of proof plaintiffs needed to hold tobacco companies accountable eluded them for years, until the connection between the asbestos in cigarette filters and lung cancer eventually was proven. Yet even there, tobacco itself was not found guilty. As the governments slowly but surely took on the responsibility for their citizens, the tobacco industry aggressively defended themselves, especially in America where criticizing tobacco companies was portrayed as an unpatriotic act. The very beginning of modern America was built on tobacco, after all, and Marlboro Man was there to remind us all of the kind of grit that reflected an essential symbol of being American. The government responded with a tepid attempt to tell people of the dangers of smoking by putting warnings on cigarette packets in the mid 1960's. In accordance with the dynamics of political special interests, the first warnings were rather tame: "Cigarette smoking may be hazardous to your health." The US population responded by smoking more cigarettes, rationalizing that most things were potentially dangerous to your health anyway, so what's the fuss.

The British government tried another tactic; not being as wedded to such concepts as freedom of economic expression, they began to limit tobacco advertising. The British responded by smoking more cigarettes. The government continued valiantly to warn the people of the dangers at hand, but mostly to no avail. A new generation of British youth, enamored with the images and personalities of rock bands such as the Beatles and the Rolling Stones, found smoking appealing. Britain was finally having some fun after years of post-war gloom.

The 1960's were an interesting time for tobacco. The war in Vietnam raged, tobacco taking its traditional wartime role—but, this time sharing the stage with other drugs, both natural and synthetic. The Chinese Revolution was in full swing, Chairman Mao smoking like a fiend, and the Chinese population, doing the best they could in the circumstances, smoked to alleviate the pangs of hunger and the instabilities due to social upheaval. Fidel Castro was making his stand against the imperialists to the north, and in the process cut off supply of the famous Cuban cigars. Both Fidel and his revolutionary compatriot Che were devoted smokers, and Fidel continued to enjoy his cigars (until recently) even allegedly avoiding being poisoned by cigars laced with botulinus toxin, courtesy of the CIA.

THE LEGAL CHALLENGE TO TOBACCO'S ASCENDANCE

By the beginning of the 1970's, the tide was beginning to turn against tobacco. In 1971, cigarette advertising was banned on American TV. In 1972, all cigarette advertisements had to carry a health warning and, in 1975, Minnesota prohibited smoking in public places and at public meetings—the first of many states to limit the freedom to smoke. A new industry was developing and a wide array of techniques and programs designed to help people give up smoking appeared in ads instead. In the UK, a relentless effort against smoking began to make an impression on the general public and the proportion of the male population who smoked fell below 50% for the first time in 50 years. An economic decline, labor unrest, and growing health concerns were all involved in this change, and although American tobacco companies renewed their interest in the British smoker (finding a useful advertising niche in Formula 1 car racing) the British didn't increase their habit much. However, what had become apparent to the marketing departments of tobacco companies was that the most crucial time to influence a potential smoker was when that potential smoker was still an adolescent—a slightly inconvenient factor, given the law prohibiting youth from smoking. Scientific research revealing the extraordinary addictiveness of nicotine was being used by both sides in the tobacco war, and the tobacco companies realized that the earlier they got tobacco into the lungs of a growing individual, the more likely they were to become attached to smoking. After all, as people grew old and died, whether or not tobacco-use had contributed to their demise, a continual stream of new customers needed to be found.

In retrospect, it still is not entirely clear that nicotine itself is as addictive as many studies claim. While scientific evidence has demonstrated the chemical's addictive potential, investigation into individuals' psychological susceptibility to addiction has not been taken far beyond traditional psychoanalytical theory, which imposes a somewhat limited perspective on the complexity of the human desire for drugs and the dynamics of addiction. Although the mechanics of nicotine addiction will be evident once a person has imbibed enough of it and has overcome the initial discomfort of taking a foul tasting poison, this doesn't explain the initial impulse that leads a person to persist in using an addictive substance long enough for addiction to occur. What purpose does it serve people to do this and how does the process change when people in different cultures, with different histories and needs, take up the habit of tobacco or any other drug?

Although historical evidence suggests that early cultures had a reverent attitude toward tobacco use, the human relationship with tobacco took a very different turn when the white man adopted the habit, and tobacco consequently touched nearly every culture of the world. As human societies have become more homogenized, the relationship with tobacco has correspondingly served similar needs—some very different than those of the first humans who came across tobacco plants some 18,000 years ago.

By the 1980's the anti-smoking league smelled victory, with the medical profession in the front line of the campaign. The British Medical Association released a report in 1984, portraying smokers as victims, due to some inherent weakness, trying to justify more punitive measures like banning smoking altogether. This flew in the face of notions of individual choice challenging certain social assumptions of autonomy, choice and responsibility as well as relegating tobacco to the status of other outlawed drugs. From the anti-smoking point of view, condemning smokers to being a social outcast or deviant is a morally appropriate position, even if they are a victim and not responsible. The governments generally settled for yet more taxation, which penalized the working classes as they remained more stubbornly loyal to smoking for obvious reasons.

The tobacco companies' refusal to admit to the dangers of tobacco also prevented them from exploring safer forms of smoking, as this would mean admitting the very danger they were denying. It kept them from researching whether smoking a limited number of cigarettes might be significantly less harmful to the average individual than smoking more. Another significant development was the recognition that not only were smokers victims because of their susceptibility to addictive substances, but non-smokers were also victimized by exposure to tobacco smoke in the air they breathed when others smoked nearby. This led to even more possibilities for the legal profession, as virtually everybody could be seen as a victim needing representation. More pressure grew to separate smokers from others, forcing them into glass cages in airports, or separate rooms in bars. For non-smokers who had always had to endure smoking in public places, this development liberated them from the personal discomfort forced upon them by the smoker's habit, the pendulum swinging yet further away from the smoker's corner. In 2005, this reached a new level when the San Francisco Board of Supervisors banned smoking in all City owned public spaces, including parks.

In the 1980's however, the tobacco companies had still not paid one cent in compensation to any smoker, let alone a non-smoker, and in spite of continued pressure, proceeded with their business, marketing their product wherever they could. One way was the film industry, paying movie producers fees for product placement so cigarette smoking and brand names could be seen throughout a movie. The tobacco companies, perhaps seeing the long-term instability of counting on cigarette sales to make their profits, began to diversify, using their considerable assets to purchase other companies in diverse fields. In the process, they became even larger influences in both American and British economies, though many would never have guessed that the cookies they were eating were made by R.J. Reynolds, or that Kraft Foods was owned by Philip Morris. American companies were also doing very well exporting their product, mainly to the developing world, and were supported by the American government and individual senators. Senator Jesse Helms, from North Carolina, was particularly enthusiastic. He helped open up the Japanese market to American tobacco companies, leading to a large increase in smoking habits there. The end of the Cold War also revealed another huge market, as millions of people were fed up with living under Soviet rule and needed some relief from the monotony of social collectivism. Thus, even as the governments of the advanced countries of the west were recognizing the harm from tobacco, and despite the growing consciousness of the social and health effects from smoking, the people of Asia, Eastern Europe and South America initially didn't have such hesitations and smoking habits continued to increase, ably supported by American tobacco companies and the "concerned" government.

A novel idea developed in the West to allow the consumer to ingest nicotine without the personal and social inconvenience of smoking – the good old American habit of chewing gum which had originally been created for the committed tobacco chewer. Knowledge of the addictiveness of nicotine was obviously incentive enough to market nicotine gum and for many it became a supply of nicotine when unable to smoke due to public inconvenience, as in airplanes and other public transport.

Another momentous event in the history of smoking occurred in the first Gulf War in 1990, when American GI's did not have cigarettes given to them as part of their rations. They had to buy their own. Cigarettes had not been in the rations of soldiers for a number of years, and although Philip Morris initially gave 2 million cigarettes to soldiers in the gulf, this was soon stopped. One other event occurred in the 1980's and 90's: the cigar became fashionable once more, this time adopted by the rich and powerful as a statement of their business acumen and largess. As the largest corporations in the world became behemoths, cigars were part of the rituals of negotiations and power deals, Cuban cigars being the first of choice. Cuba, struggling for survival after the Cold War and an ongoing embargo made their famous—and often fake—Cohibas available for cold hard cash, and the contradictory symbiosis became complete as rich capitalists adopted them as their talisman.

Strangely enough, after seeing a decline in tobacco smoking in the 1980's with the gradual demonization of cigarettes and tobacco companies, smoking became more fashionable again, rather like bell-bottom trousers. Hollywood and celebrities continued to smoke, both in life and in film, their influence growing ever stronger due to an image obsessed celebrity culture. Tobacco companies, with their fingers forever on the pulse of social trends, realized that the old image of the Marlboro man with his tough guy ways had to be modified to a more modern, caring male image, one consistent with the changing gender dynamics, environmental sensitivity and other "new age" sensibilities. This new trend was termed as "Wildering" and is described by Gately as "A new appreciation of ourselves as primal beings, returning to nature to test ourselves, physically and spiritually" which "demonstrates that the impulse that drives the cowboy myth has never been more compelling to consumers."[17] This is perhaps the same vision embodied by television programs such as "Survivor."

In England, the resurgent film industry also continually portrayed many of its characters smoking, especially women, and by the mid 1990's there was an increase in the number of women who smoked. The government had to admit that not only the trendy and glamorous were puffing again, emulating their favorite celebrities, but also single women and single mothers on the dole, of which there were about 1 million collecting income support. 55% of them smoked five packs of cigarettes a week, at 2.50 pounds a pack, spending altogether 357 million pounds on cigarettes, most of it tax. In Britain, the tax on cigarettes is about 80% of its purchase price, contributing 10.5 billion pounds to the exchequer in 1997. All in all, the government in Britain has always done very well with the tax revenue from smoking and collects far more in tax than it spends in treatment due to smoking. Smokers conveniently die a lot younger than non-smokers, relieving the country of more old people to clog up the hospitals, nursing homes and bingo halls. It has been estimated that a smoker who dies 16 years before a non-smoker (the average estimate) will save the government 250,000 pounds. Perhaps this is why Britain is one of the countries in Europe not pursuing a zero tolerance agenda as yet.

Even in America, where taxation has generally been much lower, health care costs to the country have not exceeded taxation revenue.

However, the biggest financial incentive came from the legal industry who in the 1990's began to win huge payouts to the "victims" of the tobacco companies. "In 1998, the tobacco industry reached a Master Settlement Agreement with various American states which committed it to making payments in perpetuity to cover all the states' medical expenses incurred in treating sick smokers. The total cost to the industry over a twenty-five-year period will be $246 billion...."[18] This settlement will be paid by raising the price of cigarettes.

The big winners of this settlement, though, are the lawyers representing the states. In Mississippi, lawyers will receive $1.4 billion between them, representing 35% of the total to be paid to the state for the care of sick and dying smokers. In Florida, the fees work out at $233 million per lawyer. One Florida lawyer recently won $145 billion on behalf of sick Florida smokers. The lawyer's share might make him richer than Bill Gates."[19]

As the pressure to give up cigarettes has grown in America, many people turned to another drug, Prozac, and other similar antidepressants. These drugs have become a socially acceptable way to deal with the daily strains of life, as long as you ignore the apparent connection with increased suicides and homicides associated with their use. One further example of the puritanical spirit of the anti-smoking agenda occurred when a death row inmate in Texas was refused a cigarette just before his execution on the grounds that it wasn't good for his health!

Outside of the UK and the USA, other countries have not been so keen to find tobacco companies legally and morally responsible for the health hazards of smoking. Both Spain and France have had state monopolies on tobacco, so those governments would have to be held directly responsible. However, to appease the growing anti-smoking suit, cigarette taxes have been increased in both countries, leading to a corresponding rise in cigarette smuggling, particularly in the historically rebellious Andalusia region in Southern Spain. The market for smuggled cigarettes is extraordinary. "Perhaps one-third of all internationally traded cigarettes are smuggled."[20] Countries with weak currencies have always used tobacco as a means of exchange, and differing levels of taxation invite smuggling. Smuggling is such a huge part of the tobacco economy that tobacco companies actually help facilitate the distribution of their cigarettes this way, afraid their product will be left out of the loop. In developing nations like India and China, huge numbers of people continue to smoke. China has about one-third of the world's smokers within its borders, with people from all social strata enjoying the habit. There seems to be no decline in this interest, and only time will tell whether the war against tobacco will create a smokeless world and whether that world will be any happier or healthier than the one we have now.

Chapter Three

Contemplations on the Impact of Tobacco

Tobacco has been a key factor in the evolution of the United States of America. The development by English settlers of the first tobacco plantations would ultimately lead to the revolt against English taxation on tobacco and to the American Revolution. Subsequent to that, the importation of slaves to work on tobacco plantations irrevocably changed the course of American history. The fact that another very addictive plant, sugar cane, provided the other main motive for slave importation lends metaphorical significance to the connection between addiction and slavery. Tobacco belongs to a botanical family called the Solanaceae, a group of well-known plants that includes the potato, tomato, eggplant as well as more poisonous examples. In homeopathic medicine, the most utilized remedies from this family are datura (Stramonium), henbane (Hyoscyamus) and deadly nightshade (Belladonna). These remedies share certain properties and symptoms that are characteristic of the Solanaceae family. One of the most striking qualities is the theme of good and evil, often described in the form of darkness and light. The history of tobacco use also exemplifies this theme and both dark and light sides are revealed with the experience of tobacco. The indigenous peoples of South and North America took tobacco both as a sacrament and for basic pleasure and practical use. Compared to westerners, indigenous peoples were more accepting of tobacco, understanding it as a means to connect to the spirit world. The way any substance is used is to some extent a reflection of that culture's background and mythology. The connection with the spirit world that tobacco facilitated for shamans is not dissimilar to the use of tobacco in war and circumstances in which death is near. However, in Western cultures, the attitude toward tobacco has been more ambivalent. Similar to the use of other "drugs" inherited as a result of colonization (tea, coffee, cocaine, marijuana and opium) the use of tobacco has often been curtailed, but without great success. Therefore, although all cultures using drugs suffer a similar problem with addiction and other side-effects when those substances are used (abused) enough, the consciousness and intention that people have when using drugs appears to alter their subsequent effects. If the reason for using a drug is only to escape reality and not to enhance it, then the more we try to suppress their use, the stronger they seem to become. As Gary Snyder has stated, "Those human cultures which demonize death or pain or sickness are thus less able to deal with the bitter side of nature, with intoxications; and make themselves doubly sick."

It is interesting that tobacco has often been symbolic of freedom and defiance. Castro smoking his cigars is one of the most potent symbols of defiance in modern history, whereas the struggle for women's emancipation often was symbolized by smoking cigarettes. On this topic, Frans Vermeulen in his book *Prisma, the Arcana of Materia Medica Illuminated* quotes writer Richard Klein:

> "Whereas smoking cigarettes was once an act of defiance, it is now largely an occasion for guilt, although defiance and guilt have always belonged to the psychology of cigarette smoking – forms of the violence of transgressing the interdiction of tobacco.... Like other tyrants such as Louis XIV, Napoleon and Hitler, James I despised smoking and demonized tobacco. The relation between tyranny and the repression of the right to grow, sell, use, or smoke tobacco can be seen most clearly in the way movements of liberation, revolutions both political and cultural, have always placed those rights at the center of their political demands. The history of the struggle against tyrants has been frequently inseparable from

that of the struggle on behalf of the freedom to smoke, and at no time was this more the case than during the French and American revolutions. The earliest political history of this country, from the time of the first English settlers in Virginia, who survived on the commerce of tobacco, to the revolutionary struggle against English taxes, was forged in the name of the right and freedom to grow and use tobacco – free from the impositions of the state. Governments have always sought to control the use of tobacco, for reasons that have to do with what Napoleon, the first to create a state of monopoly of tobacco, called its eminent taxability: it is a habituating luxury that even the poorest will pay for. But the reasons may also have to do with these tyrants' moralizing tendency and their allergic reaction to individual acts of expressive freedom."[1]

In the United States today (2005) we have a "war" against smoking, backed with ample evidence of its harm, and at the same time a political culture that is becoming more draconian and repressive. President George W. Bush, espousing fundamentalist Christian values (even though his own beliefs are shrouded in his own alcoholic history and political redemption story), represents a form of puritanical Christianity steeped in the polarities of good and evil, black and white, guilt and redemption. How symbolic therefore that the fight against tobacco runs parallel to this current social and political dynamic in the United States. To quote Richard Klein:

"The increase of attacks directed against smoking in the last decades could be seen as the harbinger of the wave of censorship that threatens to engulf America. Like the Gypsy dances that were banned at French carnivals, smoking cigarettes has become an act that arouses irrational fears and excessively repressive impulses, even if it deserves to be civically disapproved. Cigarettes are bad for your health, like many things that are consumed thirty times a day; perhaps they are worse than most. But historically, the laws that are devised to suppress them fail to do so, may in fact produce the opposite of what they intend and this paradox gives rise to suspicions about the motives and attitudes that underlie their imposition.

> If there is any chance that society will ever renounce tobacco, it will not be because of censorship, which will only foster its use. Not until society has glimpsed the aura of divinity behind the hideous mask will it grasp the nature of its old fascination and begin to invent new gods for these times."[2]

Interestingly, at the beginning of 2004, Ireland banned smoking in public places, including pubs. How they were able to do so, in a country with such an intrinsic pub and smoking culture, is perhaps due again to the tenacity of religious influence in the country. Anyone caught smoking in a prohibited location now faces a fine of up to 3,000 euros. It will be interesting to see how long more religiously ambivalent countries like England, Italy and Germany will last, or France with its ingrained Gaulloise and Gitanes laced culture. France attempted in October 2003 to cut smoking levels by raising the price of cigarettes by 20%, provoking a strike from furious tobacconists, many fearing being forced out of business by smokers crossing borders to buy cigarettes in neighboring countries.

An additional dimension in the war on smoking is the role of the big tobacco companies. The extraordinary power of these companies and their refusal to accept the connection between smoking and cancer has united the efforts of both progressive and conservative forces in a common spirit to curb smoking. But aside from the obvious harm that tobacco can cause, further damage from smoking stems from the many adulterants put into the tobacco by the tobacco companies, substances perhaps more toxic than the tobacco itself. Cigarettes contain more than 40 compounds that are considered carcinogens which increase the risk of developing malignancies in the larynx, oral cavity, esophagus, bladder, pancreas, kidney and stomach. Cigarettes are one of the most heavily marketed consumer products in the U.S. The American Lung Association (ALA) estimated that in 1999, tobacco companies spent almost $8.2 billion to promote and advertise their products. The ALA also estimates that smoking costs $150 billion each year in health care costs.

The tobacco companies have more recently switched their marketing focus to developing countries, especially in attracting women to smoke. Countries like China and India are seen as the next big market for these companies as their populations already have a high percentage of smokers. In China, two out of three men smoke. However, in India, the government is now taking serious measures to curb smoking.

In America, there have been suggestions in meetings of the Los Angeles City Council to ban smoking in public parks, leading one councilor to state that the city seems more concerned about a waft of second hand smoke than the smog from countless 8 lane highways. The economic influences of this debate cannot be separated from the moral argument, creating some rather strange ironies and outright hypocrisy. Klein quotes from a speech in 1990 by Louis W. Sullivan, secretary of health and human services, declaring war again on smoking: "Let this just be the beginning of an all-out effort to resist the tobacco merchant's attempts to earn profits at the expense of the health and well-being of our poor and minority citizens. This trade-off between profits and good health must stop. Enough! No more." However, at the same time, the administration was seeking to eliminate stronger controls on auto emissions from a new bill that would have put controls of toxic chemicals and improved fuel efficiency to reduce carbon dioxide in exhaust emissions, and also resisted efforts to cut emission of acid rain creating emissions from industry. The administration was also threatening Thailand with reprisals if that country implemented its ban on cigarette imports and cigarette advertising. In 1988 American exports of tobacco to Asia rose by 76% in one year alone.

In Europe, in 1989, 61% of Greek men smoked, 38% of Irish men and the rest of European men in the 40th percentile. Danish women smoked the most, at 45%, with Portuguese women the lowest at 12%. It is interesting to note that it is in countries where women have the most economic and social freedoms that smoke the most and also where cigarettes are the most expensive. In China more than 350 million people smoke—or a quarter of the population (2004). According to a 1996 survey reported by AP news agency, 112 million people smoked tobacco in India, while 96 million used tobacco products like chewing tobacco. In Russia, recent figures (2003), showed that 63% of Russian men smoked, while one in three Russians overall were addicted to cigarettes.

However, governments throughout the world have gone on the offensive. On the BBC website of May 31st, 2004, it was stated that in Australia smokers will no longer be able to light up on Manly, one of Australia's most famous and picturesque stretches of surfing beach. Other beaches are considering following suit. In India, recent laws have banned direct or indirect advertising of tobacco products and the sale of cigarettes to children. Anyone caught breaking the law will be fined 200 rupees ($.4.50). Iran banned smoking in public buildings and advertising in October 2003, but both measures have had little effect. Tanzania banned smoking in many public places in July 2003, with smoke free zones declared on public transport, as well as in schools and hospitals.

Has tobacco had its time?

It seems the right thing to do. Governments should pursue the tobacco companies and their dubious ethics, but can this be done without denying people the desire to imbibe some kind of "poison"? If not tobacco, then what? Doesn't every society need its own particular poison? Can we create cleaner tobacco, one that isn't full of chemical toxins? Or are the toxins just part of the play of poison that tobacco attracts and that attracts humans to tobacco? Can we change our consciousness in the way we use tobacco? Can we cultivate it and use it without chemically manipulating it and abusing it? Can tobacco again be seen as a symbol of life, communication and calmness, or only as the malevolent poison it has proven to be? Are we reaping the revenge of tobacco for having so abused and adulterated it? Has the day of tobacco come and gone.

In other cultures, smoking was originally a ritual, a form of ceremony, a means of bonding and connecting. In western culture it has become more of a lonely ritual, expressing a more desperate need to suck in the fire of tobacco, to suppress the emotions that challenge us in our lives – although forcing New Yorkers to smoke outside of bars and restaurants, even in winter, has forged new bonds of ritual inhaling. The 'Malboro' Man has been the most potent image of tobacco for the modern man, a metaphor of the pioneering spirit of America with its parallel individualism.

In Native American cultures, tobacco was smoked in pipes, made from stones, with tobacco mixed with other substances. In a chapter of a book called *Further Dimensions of Healing Addictions,* author Donna Cunningham, writes a chapter on tobacco, and states that:

> "The stones from which pipes were traditionally made were themselves transmitters of the energy of tobacco and other smoked substances, part of the ritual and part of what made them effective. They acted as crucibles for releasing the essence of the plant. Pipe smokers who make a fetish of collecting pipes dimly remember this. In different parts of the world, different plants were burned, and different stones were used for the pipes. Meerschaum might have been used in one area, flint in another and ivory elsewhere. In Black Elk's book, The Sacred Pipe, the smoking rites of one group, the Siouix, are discussed."

> "The stones naturally occurring in an area acted on the native plants to meet the needs of the native dwellers. Orientals used jade and alabaster as containers for their incense, not just because such containers were lovely to behold, but also because they worked with the substances they burned. Native Americans traditionally use abalone shells to burn sage. If you burn sage, other incenses, or tobacco, you might do well to imitate our spiritual elders and burn them in stone holders."[3]

Perhaps the most significant event in the last 500 years has been the ability for different cultures to meet and interrelate. Historically, this has been mainly motivated by imperial and colonial agendas of the European powers, dominating regions of the world and their peoples for many years. However, as a consequence, we now have a situation in which the evolution and history of disparate cultures and societies are firmly wedded together, creating a unique mosaic of cultural, political and social influences in most countries of the world. This has been mostly clearly written about in the work of writers such as Edward Said in classic texts such as Orientalism.

The relationship of oppressor/perpetrator and victim is a complex one, which can be explored in both individual instances as well as in national dimensions. Many of those colonized countries are still paying the price for these events, with the majority of African, South American and Middle Eastern countries "created" by the colonizers as they carved up areas for economic exploitation. However, it can be speculated that there is always a price to pay for this kind of oppression, a debt is owed to those people that have been exploited. This debt may take many forms and the amount of debt may be predicated by the willingness of the colonizers to accept responsibility for what they have done.

One way in which this debt may be being paid is through the drugs that have been introduced to the colonizer's countries from the colonized. Tobacco, Cannabis, Opium, Cocaine, Coffee and Tea are the most obvious examples of drugs that are now ubiquitous in western culture, all coming as a result of colonial agendas. As a culture, are we now "victim" to the power of these drugs, heavily under their influence as we still struggle with acceptance of what we have done in the name of economic exploitation, religion and other rationalizations. Are we racing around in futile activity as we imbibe more coffee and tea to stimulate our minds and bodies to yet more action, yet seemingly unable to appreciate the moments we have? Has the coffee culture now reached its apogee with the ubiquitous spread of Starbucks to most corners of most cities in most parts of the world, creating a redundancy in its very repetition? Have cocaine and heroin eroded the core of the most vulnerable parts of our society, with the violence and corruption surrounding the drug culture and the futility of our governments to address the roots of the condition? Instead, vast resources are spent in attempting to purge drugs from the streets, refusing to acknowledge that it is not drugs that are the problem, but the institutional (spiritual) problems of the culture that stimulates this need. Is this the price we are now paying on some kind of "karmic" level?

And finally tobacco, more prevalent than the others apart from coffee and now taken up by both colonizers and the colonized. But it is still only in cultures more politically and socially systematized that tobacco has such a lure, societies that have bought the delusion of Man's separation from the world in which we live. This may be tobacco's message: Separate yourselves from the source of the earth at your own peril. We may have given the Native American cultures alcohol, and we know how much that has damaged them, but they gave us tobacco. Which has been worse? We are talking here as much about a spiritual condition as physical. We can see how the level of consciousness we bring to the use of many substances influences its impact. The commercialization of tobacco production and consumption has reflected a cultural mindset, one that has removed itself from the natural world and that sees nature's products as a means of exploitation, not of harmonious cooperation. Western cultures perhaps haven't understood the nature of tobacco and therefore used it mainly as a means to suppress strong emotions, not as a sacrament.

SMOKING FACTS

- On average each cigarette shortens a smoker's life by 11 minutes.
- People younger than 65 account for almost half of all smoking-related deaths.
- In 1965, 52% of men and 33% of women smoked; today the rate is 25% for men and 21% for women.
- Smokers are 29% more likely to suffer from asthma than are nonsmokers.
- The Centers for Disease Control (CDC) estimates that 43,000 people in the United States lose their lives each year due to smoking related diseases.
- 46.5 million adults were current smokers in 2000
- 87% of lung cancers are related to tobacco.
- Smoking in pregnancy increases the risk of premature births by 30%.
- Smoking is responsible for an estimated 30% of all cancer deaths, 21% of deaths from coronary heart disease: 18% of stroke deaths: and 82% of deaths from chronic obstructive pulmonary disease.
- Smokers lose more teeth than non-smokers.

THE ATTRACTIONS OF SMOKING: THE SWEET TASTE OF DEATH AND LIBERATION

If tobacco is reduced to its potential for harm, the obvious conclusion is that people should not smoke, but as has already been explored, the value of any action is far greater than merely its health risks. Tobacco, more than any other plant, has come to represent the polarity and contradictions of the human impulse to imbibe poisons, to explore and to alter reality according to our wishes—or the drug's. Every drug serves a purpose in this exploration, and each one has its price. To quote Richard Klein again:

> If cigarettes were not also good for you, so many good people would not have spent some part of their lives doing them uninterruptedly, often compulsively – them, or some drug or other. One thinks of the many great men and women who have died prematurely from having smoked too much: it does them an injustice to suppose that their greatness did not depend in some degree on the wisdom and pleasure and spiritual benefit they took in a habit they could not abandon. And the same could be said of others. Healthism in America has sought to make longevity the principal measure of a good life. To be a survivor is to acquire moral distinction. But another view, a dandy's perhaps, would say that living, as distinct from surviving, acquires its value from risks and sacrifices that tend to shorten life and hasten dying. A life, in that view, is judged by the suicide it commits.[4]

Jean Paul Sartre spent many years smoking, giving it up only to again take up the "demon" habit for the next 40 years. He stated that a life without smoking was not worth living. He wrote the following description of his attempt at giving up smoking, as quoted by Klein:

> "A few years ago, I was led to decide to stop smoking. The beginning was rough, and in truth, I did not so much care for the taste of tobacco that I was going to lose, as for the meaning of the act of smoking. A whole crystallization had taken place. I used to smoke at performances, mornings at work, evenings after dinner, and it seemed to me that in ceasing to smoke I was going to subtract some of the interest of the performance, some of evening dinner's savor, some of the fresh vivacity of the morning's work. Whatever unexpected event might have struck my eyes, it seemed to me that it was fundamentally impoverished as soon as I could no longer welcome it by smoking. To-be- susceptible-to-be-encountered-by-me-while-smoking: that was the concrete quality that had been universally

spread over things. And it seemed to me that I was going to tear it away from them and that, in the midst of this universal impoverishment, life was a little less worth living...."[5]

At the end of his life, Satre still smoked and drank and one day collapsed in the street. Simone de Beauvoir wrote that:

"He was told that he could save his legs only by giving up tobacco. If he did not smoke anymore, his state could be much improved and he could be assured of a quiet old age and a normal death. Otherwise his toes would have to be cut off, then his feet, and then his legs. Sartre seemed impressed. Liliane and I took him home without too much difficulty. As for tobacco, he said he wanted to think it over....
We spent the evening reading and talking. He made up his mind to stop smoking the next day, Monday. I said 'Doesn't it make you sad to think you're smoking your last cigarette?' 'No. To tell you the truth I find them rather disgusting now."[6]

However, that disgust didn't last long and he soon went back to smoking heavily.

Another Frenchman, Theodore de Banville, exponent of the Parnassian school of "l'art pour l'art", much admired by Baudelaire, wrote a piece on cigarettes in which he describes the aesthetics of the life of the dandy. Klein describes it as follows:

"The dandy aims to be able to do what he does for its own sake, not for any profit with which it might enhance his personal interests. Smoking is such a worthless, unproductive activity that it lends itself to becoming the whole purpose of life – if life it to be justified aesthetically, and not according to some utilitarian principle."[7]

Klein quotes Banville:

"In a word, everyone wants everything; however, the cigarette, which is the most imperious, the most engaging, the most demanding, the most loving, the most refined of mistresses, tolerates nothing which is not her, and compromises with nothing; it inspires a passion that is absolute, exclusive, ferocious like gambling or reading." "The smoker of cigarettes must always, at each instant, have two hands free and lips also; he can therefore be neither someone ambitious, nor a worker, nor, with a very few exceptions, a poet or an artist; every task is forbidden him, even the ineffable pleasure of screwing."[8]

Therefore tobacco, like other poisons, serves a spiritual purpose, a space in which the lustful insatiability of the mind is tamed into submission, in which there is no other desire, no wish for anything. The mere act of smoking a cigarette is a statement of that intention, to stop time and it's connection to becoming, to acquiring and to achieving. It is a respite, albeit brief, against the current of life's activities, a point of transition, which then demands its own repetition. That is the nature of a habit. To quote Sartre from Klein's book:

> "Tobacco is a symbolically "appropriated" being, since it is destroyed following the rhythm of my breath by a manner of "continuous destruction," since it passes in me and its changing into myself manifests itself symbolically by the transformation of the consumed solid into smoke. The bond between the landscape seen while smoking and this little crematorial sacrifice was such, as we have just seen, that the latter was like a symbol of the former. It therefore signified that the destructive appropriative action of tobacco was symbolically equivalent to an appropriate destruction of the entire world. Through the tobacco I was smoking it was the world that was burning, that was being smoked, that reabsorbed itself in steam to reenter in me…."[9]

Klein makes observations in his book, which parallel experiences in the homeopathic proving, in the experience of tobacco as a transitory state, a point between two places.

He states "Like writing, smoking belongs to that category of action that falls in-between the states of activity and passivity."[6] "Cigarettes have something like the capacity of incense to connect the earth to the sky and hence to invite the smoker's spirit to turn away from the negativity of the here and now toward some higher realm—some general perspective from which to view the horror all around."[11] This last quote, taken from the context of the use of cigarettes by soldiers in war describes perhaps the time of the most intimate relationship we have with cigarettes; when faced with death, they give us the calmness and the solace to face the horror, to relinquish the shrieks of anguish of our imminent demise. By tasting a little bit of death in a cigarette, it relieves us of the reality of the situation.

> You ask what we need to win this war. I will tell you, we need tobacco, more tobacco—even more than food.
>
> —General John J. Pershing to the Minister of War.

To quote Klein:

> "The last cigarette smoked before an execution is not equivalent to a shot of morphine; it stiffens the spine of the person condemned, kills escape, and promotes a resignation to necessity that gives one courage to endure the worst. It is because a moment out of time is born and then made to die that the cigarette serves as a simulcrum, a little enactment of death. It is as if the last cigarette plays out, in a controlled fiction, the death that is anticipated and feared...."[12]

This description describes cigarettes as a homeopathic dose of death, a simillimum to the reality of death. To take this connection to death a little further, Klein refers to the essay *Beyond the Pleasure Principle* by Freud. To quote:

> "What he calls the "death instinct," which underlies the pleasure principle, organizes the otherwise intermittent and wildly modulating discharges of the organism into repetitive, predictable patterns. By smoking a cigarette, ingesting a certain quantity of nicotine, the organism is hastening its death, is producing in itself more noxious effects than if it endured the discomfort of anxiety. But the death it is hastening is its own death; it substitutes its own path toward death for the process over which it otherwise has no control. Using cigarettes to master anxiety may be understood as preferring a certain form of dying over an intolerable form of living. In that respect, it is a heroic activity, not nutritive or therapeutic at all. Under some circumstances, giving oneself more discomfort is preferable to passively enduring less; assuming a death of one's own choosing is more desirable than suffering a life over which one has no control. The only thing worse than war is to lose one's freedom."[13]

To take the homeopathic parallel further, Klein then says,

> "But the physiological effect of nicotine has two stages. It not only raises blood pressure and pulse at the price of increasing discomfort—in the next moment it lowers them, producing a marked feeling of release and relief. After mastering anxiety by increasing it, by giving it a precise, punctual origin, at the cost of more intense displeasure the organism that has taken a puff of its cigarette gets a little reward for its heroism; the sudden burst of unease that accompanies the ingestion of the poison is followed by a moment of release as the organism relaxes the tension that the poison, now eliminated, had initially provoked...."[14]

THE TIBETANS AND TOBACCO

It is interesting to read the following treatise on tobacco from a Tibetan Buddhist perspective. Given the genetic similarities between the Tibetans and the Native American people of North America there is a seemingly opposite reaction to tobacco and smoking. Perhaps it has something to do with the fact that tobacco is indigenous to one culture and not to the other, or perhaps it reflects a traditional religious aversion to smoking, similar to the attitude of other religions.

Tobacco

'the guide that leads the blind on a false path which ends in a precipice' —Kyabjé Jigdrèl Yeshé Dorje, Düd'jom Rinpoche

Introduction by Ngala Rig'dzin Dorje

My Root Lamas, Ngak'chang Rinpoche and Khandro Déchen, urgently requested that I should make this text available to as many people as possible. They had been searching for this text for some years, and I was fortunate enough to be able to procure it for them – after long research. They also asked me to introduce the text on the basis of my knowledge of the ways in which Western people think. I am extremely happy to say that I have been able to provide an increasing number of people with Tibetan purification medicine and guidance for the purpose of giving up smoking.

I sincerely hope that the wider circulation of this text by His Holiness Düd'jom Rinpoche will provide a turning point for anyone who is seriously interested in Vajrayana practice—because to smoke and imagine oneself to be a practitioner is a sad contradiction. Vajrayana would appear to be unique in considering tobacco, as well as narcotics, not simply harmful to physical health but also severely damaging with regard to spiritual health. It is particularly damaging with regard to the rTsa-rLung system and renders any kind of formless practices worthless. Ngak'chang Rinpoche once said: "Those smokers who engage in silent sitting, merely sit in a cloud of smoke of which they are entirely unaware—and in which they remain entirely unaware."

In this crucial essay on the subject, HH Düd'jom Rinpoche explains the non-ordinary visionary history which illuminates the deleterious nature of these poisonous substances, according to gTérma revelations. To help Vajrayana practitioners understand the danger of smoking, HH Düd'jom Rinpoche collected major salient pronouncements of Padmasambhava concerning tobacco and narcotics for those who regard these sacred revelations as their refuge. Warnings about tobacco and narcotics have been revealed as gTérmas since early on in Tibet, by the great gTértöns, and so no authentic Nyingma practitioner need assume that what is presented here is not applicable to them. Warnings about tobacco and narcotics actually cross the spectrum of Vajrayana lineages, and advice on the subject is voluminous. The visionary accounts presented here deal with demonic intentionality, and ideas such as these may be 'difficult' for some people who are new to the practice of Vajrayana. We would therefore ask anyone who has difficulty in relating to such revelations to consider why this warning has not been more widespread within the Buddhist world. It cannot be that HH Düd'jom Rinpoche is not widely known and universally respected within the Tibetan Buddhist world. We would also ask why it is that, in the face of massive medical evidence, people still smoke – and why governments who are happy to legislate against all manner of things, find themselves unable to ban this substance. How can this be, in view of the fact that the very same governments have made it mandatory for tobacco products and tobacco advertising to carry a health warning? Is there any other non-medically prescribed substance on the open market which carries a health warning – let alone such dire warnings as are found with regard to tobacco? How is it that this substance remains legal? How is it that children can be exposed to cigarette fumes without this being regarded as 'child abuse' – when it has been shown that 'secondary smoke' is as harmful as direct smoking? We live in societies where social agencies have become extremely sensitive to such issues – so why is there not as much concern about injury from smoking with regard to children as there is concern over firearms? Surely death is death – whatever the cause, and a demon is a demon by any other name. The 'demonic quality' of tobacco is evident whether or not one perceives the 'demon'. The important fact here, for anyone who has respect and devotion for HH Düd'jom Rinpoche, is that smoking destroys one's practice and one's samaya. HH Düd'jom Rinpoche is the Lama whom most other Nyingma Lamas alive today venerate as the epitome of all that is inspiring – so those who have not yet been convinced as to the effects of smoking, please take this opportunity to rid yourself of its corrupting influence.

Chapter Four

Commentaries on Tobacco and the Proving

LIFE AND DEATH

"Deathly" nausea is one of the well-known characteristics of Tabacum. The word death is interesting in relation to this substance. The facts of tobacco use are testament to its toxicity and its impact on societies throughout the world. It is the most widely used drug known to man, having spread originally from the Americas to the rest of the world. Its use is now strongest in developing countries, although in Europe a large percentage of people still smoke. Tobacco lingers around the beginnings and endings of life like no other substance. It is often a witness of the moments after birth or just before death. For a father after the birth of his child or a soldier about to go to battle, a cigarette is the companion often sought: the last rites before an execution are associated with smoking a cigarette. Nicotiana plants are frequently seen in cemeteries, reinforcing the connection between tobacco and the other world.

A common feeling with tobacco is one of calmness, as it collects the mind and allows clear thinking. The proving demonstrated a clear affinity with transitions between one state and another, between sleep and waking, that in-between state when the soul is in no-man's land. Similar to the moment before death or just after birth, it is a time of movement from one realm to another, from dark to light or light to dark, a state of movement, a journey. The transition between heaven and earth is also seen in the proving, a "sinking" down, into the earth or a "floating" above, "rising" beyond the earth.

This connection between life and death is evidenced in the dreams of the provers. Some dreamt of births or babies while others dreamt of people dying and of funerals. Dale Pendell writes:

> Tobacco has to do with energy. Transferring energy, attuning energy. As such, energy being traditionally godly province, tobacco is the food of the gods. Even gods have to eat, after all. And remember that tobacco is very food-like. Taking tobacco relieves hunger, much like food does. Further, tobacco grows in gardens, just like food. It likes gardens. It likes rich, sunny soil, and will even volunteer if you prepare a spot for it ... Tobacco is probably the oldest cultigen in North America.... So we have a plant that looks like food, grows where food grows, allays hunger but still is not quite food. That is, tobacco allays hunger but only temporarily: eventually you still have to eat real food. And tobacco brings its own hunger, a craving that is analogous to the hunger for food. Given these premises, deducing that tobacco is indeed food, but spirit food rather than human food, is not so far-fetched... The gods' problem is that although they need to eat, just as we do, no food grows in the spirit land. So they have to deal with humans, who have the tobacco monopoly. They have to bargain. In exchange for our feeding them, and enduring the hardships that such feeding entails, they will try to help us out on their side: keeping accidents from happening, diverting disasters, spilling the beans about where certain animals are living and who it was that pilfered the fish traps, and generally acting as diplomats between various, often malevolent, spirits. So the spirits let us know when they are hungry: the craving of nicotine withdrawal is the growling stomach of the hungry spirit. We feed them by taking tobacco ourselves, and a transference takes place. Some Shamans smoke tobacco more or less continuously.[1]

Donna Cunningham writes:

> The nature of smoke is to move freely, building bridges between different points in the reality structure. In the body, tobacco creates bridges between different chakras, bridges that shift and bend at different times. The root chakra is involved. Notice how you can light up a cigarette anytime, anyplace, and feel at home with yourself in a moment. The solar plexus can become involved. Think of all those smoke-filled conference rooms, with people using their solar plexus energy for the work process. Obviously the throat chakra is involved, as the throat is the entryway into the body of this substance, so there's an attempt to open up communication – to have a pow-wow. The third eye is part of this bridging, intuitive flashes emerging from this smoky cloud of the unconscious. Those who inhale smoke second-hand, such as the children of heavy smokers, also experience these shifts in consciousness routinely, growing up without clear awareness that this shifting is not the usual way of functioning.[2]

Near death states are also seen in the symptomatology of Tabacum as well as in the use of tobacco. States of coma, unconsciousness, presentiment and fear of death are all seen in the remedy.

COMPARISON WITH TABACUM AND OTHER DRUGS.

The remedy Tabacum has been a well-known remedy in homeopathy for a long time. However, its usage has been predominantly for physical conditions, mostly relating to nausea, vomiting, heart problems and vertigo. A more nuanced image of its psychological sensations has not been elicited. A study of the original provings show that most information of the remedy comes from the toxicological effect of the substance. There were no provings of the remedy in a high potency.

Interestingly, one of the keynote symptoms of Tabacum is a sinking feeling, usually associated with nausea. This was confirmed in the N. rustica proving, but the feeling of sinking was also seen in its psychological sensations, making it a theme of the remedy. The sinking was explained in different ways, from a falling from a high place into the earth, a falling through space, a general sinking feeling in the body. The sinking feeling was confirmed in the stomach/abdomen region. The vertigo symptoms were confirmed and also elaborated on with N. rustica. This falling, sinking feeling was consistent throughout the remedy picture, and more modalities were confirmed than are currently found with Tabacum.

Therefore, one of the most significant features of this proving is the development of the sinking feeling, from a physical keynote associated with nausea and seasickness to a metaphorical theme of the remedy, consistent with other Solanaceae and also with the shamanic use of the tobacco plant. One dream that the author had 2 days after the proving began reveal this theme: "I was on a bicycle and I flew off the top of something. It was very high and I went a long way. It was quite scary and very real. I ended up landing on a hill and was OK but was very surprised to find myself alright." In another part of the dream "I was writing and then fell into the dirt, I picked myself up and carried on writing."

One distinction between tobacco and other solanaceae is that the sinking feeling is also connected to a floating, a rising above sensation. It is not only in the direction of going toward the darkness therefore, but in rising toward the light, with a sense of surrealness and disconnection with the body. While the former state makes one think of the "darker" solanaceae, those substances whose poisons are very strong, the latter state makes one consider the other "drug" remedies such as Cannabis, Peyote and Ayahuasca, to which Tobacco is a good friend. Cannabis generally doesn't take you to totally other realms, it magnifies things in this particular realm or creates a split between this realm and another (feelings of unreality, losing control, confusion of identity). It shows you what is, but that can be scary enough, especially when you feel you are losing control of this realm, and perhaps your sanity. Peyote generally soothes you into other realms, making you feel connected and secure. It establishes trust in the nature of things, and although it can look like Cannabis in the homeopathic remedy image, it acts differently. Ayahuasca, on the other hand, along with Psilocybin and also LSD to a lesser extent, does both. It takes you to other realms, shows you the nature of other realities, which can scare the life out of you or gives you joy and connection. In experiencing other realities you have to leave this realm, which can give an experience similar to death. In the proving of Ayahuasca by Nancy Herrick, in *Sacred Plants, Human Voices,* the theme of death is stated, along with sensations of aggression and blackness. Other themes included that of Supernatural, Flow/Expansion/Power, Flying/Birds and High/Low. Most of these themes are also consistent in the Nicotiana proving, revealing perhaps the influence of the harmaline alkaloids, found in both substances. This also may reflect the essential difference between Nicotiana tabacum and Nicotiana rustica, the former not containing the harmaline alkaloids. It is interesting to note that in the proving of Ayahuasca by Herrick, one sees a certain polarity in the symptoms experienced, similar to many other drug remedies. On the one side you have death, darkness, fear and the supernatural, moving on to expansion, flying, stimulated states. In the proving, there is overall more attention given to the darker side of the symptom picture than the "higher" more ecstatic, trance like qualities of the remedy, which is a significant part of the experience of people who take Ayahuasca. The meaning of Ayahuasca varies but is often translated as vine of the dead, bitter death, or vine of the soul. The term was apparently given by the Quichua (Quecha) people of South America, who when they first used Ayahuasca did not understand its power, leading to some fatal overdoses.

It is worth mentioning that many remedies, especially drug remedies, show strongly alternating states, or opposite qualities. This is most clearly seen in the remedy picture of Opium, and has been commented on by many homeopaths. Opium is one of the main drug remedies in which the primary effect is to sedate a person. Most drug remedies used in homeopathy—Cannabis Indica, Anhalonium, Cocaine, Coffea, Thea, Piper Methysticum, Agaricus etc, stimulate in their primary action when given in a material dose and gives us most of our symptoms for the remedies. Opium on the other hand often sedates but as is seen in the materia medica it can have a stimulative effect, showing an alternating or polarized state simultaneously. Most other drugs tend to do one first before the other. One important factor here is the effect of the physiological dose of a drug remedy on a person, which often creates some confusion as to its effect. Most drugs if taken in enough quantity will sedate an individual, but in relatively small amounts they will stimulate. This is seen in studying the effects of tobacco. Shamans would take enough to induce unconsciousness, to create a death like state as a spiritual practice, whereas tobacco taken in smaller amounts stimulates by focusing the mind, creating calmness. It is generally a very different reaction to the more psychoactive states induced by Cannabis, Anhalonium or Ayahuasca, but when those are taken in strong enough doses, they tend to also sedate and subdue a person.

This observation can be said to be an example of the Arndt-Schultz law which states: *"Every stimulus on a living cell elicits an activity which is inversely proportional to the intensity of the stimulus." Arndt stated that "weak stimuli slightly accelerate the vital activity, middle-strong stimuli raise it, strong ones suppress it and very strong ones halt it."* The differing action of strong physiological and weak physiological doses of many substances are examples of this law and are also seen in homeopathic provings when the substances are given in varying material doses. It is worth emphasizing that the Arndt-Schultz law is still dealing with physiological (material) doses, albeit in sub-toxic amounts, and not in homeopathically potentized amounts. The uniqueness of this in drug remedies is that many people take these substances in many different doses and although they are not poisonous in the sense that some plant remedies are, they're effect on human consciousness is a complex one. Furthermore, substances given in such subtoxic amounts reflect both the initial effect of the substance and the secondary effect of the "vitality" of the subject being given the substance.

This phenomenon is observed clearly in the symptomatology of drug remedies and the proving data gleaned from the empirical experience with these substances. As has been mentioned, some of the most significant symptoms used to prescribe drug remedies are taken from the use of these substances in a material dose, not in the effect of potentized drugs given in provings. However, what the Arndt-Schultz law reveals is similar to provings in that small doses (both subtoxic and potentized doses) are a mix of the primary and secondary effect of the substance and of the prover. The Arndt-Schultz law is dealing with a specific stimulative reaction to the impact of the substance, as opposed to the more non-specific (general) reaction of the whole organism to the proving substance.

Samuel Hahnemann, the founder of Homeopathy, spoke about the primary and secondary effect of medicines, both in homeopathic and allopathic doses. As is understood in the homeopathic action of a substance, the primary effect is essentially the stimulative dynamic of the remedy given, mostly imperceptible to the patient unless an aggravation occurs. The aggravation is still essentially part of the primary effect, although obviously part of the body's reactive mechanism. The secondary effect is the healing reaction of the vital force to that primary stimulus. However, in material doses the primary effect is the initial physiological impact of the substance, e.g. a numbing of pain when an opiate is given, and the secondary effect is an increase in pain when it wears off. Hahnemann spoke exhaustively to this when discussing the palliative effects of crude (allopathic/antipathic) drugs. However, when a remedy is given in a potentized dose, the primary effect is only stimulative to the vital force; it doesn't act in any other way and its effect is conditional on the homeopathicity of the case.

Another way to look at this is to study the symptomatology of drug remedies. Many of the symptoms express the experience of taking the substance in a physical (primary) dose. It is the excitability of Coffea, the feelings of power of Coca, the theoretical loquacity of Cannabis that gives us our image of the remedy. The following is a quote of a "crude" proving of Tabacum, as stated in Allen's Encyclopedia, Clarke's Dictionary and other materia medicas:

> *He went to sleep in the cabin, which was full of large packages of tobacco, but was harassed by wild and frightful dreams, and suddenly awaked about midnight, bathed in a cold dew, and totally unable to speak or move.*
>
> *He knew, however, perfectly where he was, and recollected everything that had occurred the preceding day; he could not*

make any bodily effort whatever, and tried in vain to get up, or change his position.

The watch on deck struck four bells, and he counted them, though it seemed to him as if he did not hear the beat, but received the vibration through his body.

About this time a seaman came into the cabin with a light, and carried away an hour-glass without observing the sufferer.

Shortly after a pane of glass was broken in the skylight, and he saw the fragments of glass drop on the floor.

These circumstances which really occurred, are mentioned to show that Mr. H. experienced real sensations, and was not still under the influence of perturbed dreams.

His inability to move was not accompanied by any pain or uneasiness, but he felt as if the principle of life had entirely departed from his frame.

At length he became totally insensible, and continued so till an increase of wind made the sea a little rough, which caused the vessel to roll.

The motion, he supposes, had the effect of awakening him from his trance, and he contrived somehow or other to get up and go on deck.

His memory was totally lost for about a quarter of an hour; he knew that he was in a ship, but nothing more.

While in this state he observed a man drawing water from the sea in buckets, and requested him to pour one on his head.

On the seaman doing so, all his faculties were immediately restored, and he acquired a most vivid recollection of a vast variety of ideas and events which appeared to have passed through his mind, and to have occupied him during the time of his supposed insensibility.[3]

All the symptoms above can be attributable to the primary action of tobacco even though there are some alternating symptoms apparent in this picture (the sudden clarity after the stupefied state).

CLINICAL COMPARISONS

Another remedy to compare Nicotiana rustica with is Lobelia inflata, commonly called Indian Tobacco. This remedy is not part of the same botanical family but part of the Campanulales, a sub-family of the Asteridae family. Similar to the tabacums, it has the deathly nausea, along with vertigo and vomiting and often with profuse salivation. It has the profuse sweat, often cold, with a faintness and weakness in the epigastric region. It has a fear of imminent death and most significantly, much difficulty in respiration with rattling and no expectoration, which distinguishes it from the tabacums. It is one of the remedies to consider in respiratory conditions such as asthma, coughs and emphysema, especially when the feeling is that they have been smoking too much tobacco.

Two other remedies intimately connected with Tobacco are Spigelia (pinkroot) and Caladium seguinum (american arum). Both remedies are indicated based on an aggravation from tobacco as well as for their desire for it. In fact, studying the symptoms of both remedies reveals very similar effects of having taken too much tobacco and also with some of the symptoms from the proving. Spigelia has a great affinity for the heart and for the nerves of the face, eyes and the left side. It is one of the most indicated remedies in prosopalgia and other neuralgic conditions of the face and eye. The symptomatology of Tabacum also shows neuralgic symptoms in the face, with pain, tearing and numbness. In the proving of N. rustica, there were distinct symptoms of pain, tingling and neuralgic sensations. Similarly, the affinity for eye conditions in Spigelia were also seen in the proving, with symptoms of lachrymation, pain, general sensitiveness of eyes, blurred vision etc. The heart symptoms are strong in both Spigelia and Tabacum, and the proving of N. rustica also revealed some heart and chest symptoms. One other interesting observation is the correspondence between Tobacco and other remedies in the Logonaceae family, including Spigelia as well as Nux vomica, Ignatia, Gelsemium and Strychnine. All these remedies have an aggravation from tobacco.

Caladium has an affinity for the heart, and is listed in the rubric, *Chest, tobacco heart.* It is noted for its desire, aversion and aggravation from tobacco. Caladium has intense itching in the genitalia and a heightened sexual state that can also be seen both in Tabacum and the proving of N. rustica. Caladium has this state of nervous excitation, which the books describe as "restless, cannot control himself after smoking." This heightened state can be seen as one of one of the primary effects of taking tobacco, and is revealed more in the proving of N. rustica than the symptoms of Tabacum. The mental state of Tabacum reveals more the lower, more sedative effect of taking tobacco.

TOBACCO AND OTHER SOLANACEAE.

The plants of the same botanical family may share certain symptom characteristics, some more than others. One goal therefore is to explore what is common to the overall family and what is characteristic to each remedy. The Solanaceae vary widely in their homeopathic pictures and their actual usage, from the highly poisonous and intoxicating Stramonium and Belladonna to the more benign red pepper (*Capsicum)*, Potato (*Solanum Tuberosum)* and Tomato (*Lycopersicum)*.

The following themes are some of the well-known ones in the Solanaceae family, especially that of Stramonium, Belladonna, Hyoscyamus and Mandragora, the "darker remedies of the family."

The dark – evil, monsters, dark and deep water, black.

Fears – horror, violence, dark, terror, torture, suffocation, alone, abandoned, persecution, shining objects.

Persecution – feeling threatened, violated, stalked, abused, jealousy, forsaken, concentration camps.

Forsaken – alone, anguish, cold and alone, religious abandonment.

Violence – Sudden, shock, exploding, threatening and being threatened, tortured, knives, cutting, striking, cruelty, death.

The unconscious – Nightmares, the unknown, ghosts, snakes, evil, witches, sex, hell, religion, praying, other worlds.

Divided – body separated, divided into two, buried, distorted, split.

Intensity – sudden reactions, sharp, shooting, throbbing pains, inflammations, near death, jerking, convulsions, spasms.

Suffocation – constriction, pressure, buried, tunnels, escape, congestion, blood.

Strength – power, rage.

Every remedy has its dark side, the psychological depths to which the remedy can go. With the Solanaceae, the dark side is dark indeed, full of intensity and violence, pain, despair and horror. Images from the movie *Apocalypse Now* express the feelings seen with the Solanaceae– "The horror, the horror."

One can imagine the worst fears of a Stramonium, or to put it another way, what would be guaranteed to produce a Stramonium state. In the 1988 Dutch film *Spoorloos* ("The Vanishing") after a man's wife has been kidnapped he persuades the kidnapper to show him what he did with his wife. He then wakes up buried alive in a coffin, under the ground. Imagine what that would feel like – alone, cold, dark, suffocating, full of terror, the air running out as you dig into the wood with your nails. One could imagine the Belladonna state, being tied up, bandaged head to foot or constricted in a box where you can't move, or just enough to thrash about without getting out; or the Hyoscyamus state, being left all alone, deserted by everybody or surrounded by snakes or people trying to kill you. You might well think that witches are surrounding you, similar to the Hyoscyamus state that most of Europe was in during the Middle Ages when hundreds of thousands, if not millions of women were burnt at the stake for being witches. Entire villages were emptied of their women. In all three remedies, when faced with this threat, the tendency is to thrash out, to become excited, intense, violent and to escape.

On the individual level, the dynamic of the Solanaceae is an interplay between the unconscious forces of the human mind, that reservoir of feelings, thoughts and unresolved issues that lie suppressed, ignored and unintegrated into the realm of human consciousness. Fear of the unknown and the threat of the dark forces of the universe, drives a person to seek the light as a refuge from the threat of what is unknown or misunderstood. On a cultural level, the inability of a society to acknowledge the complexity of the forces that threaten to rear up and pollute its most potent symbols and myths—those representing its own notions of truth, good and innocence—creates a split in the collective psyche, a polarization between good and evil, dark and light, Heaven and Hell. Evil is projected onto taboo images, all seen as external threats to the sanctity of innocence and "truth".

So where is Tobacco then? Tobacco could be seen to be the pathway, the potentiator and communicator between the two worlds; the dark world of Stramonium, Belladonna, Hyoscyamus and Mandragora and the lighter world of Capsicum, Solanum nigrum, Lycopersicum and Solanum tuberosum. Tobacco is the facilitator between opposites, it attempts to liberate from constriction, to help the journey up and down the spiral of life, to be a bridge in those transitional moments. Like the other Solanaceae, death is not far away, but tobacco forces us to respect it and see it for what it is. It doesn't appreciate being tamed and manipulated. Using it just to suppress fear and anger has its price—death, the ultimate price.

Tobacco is therefore the in-between state, the crack of the earth opening up in an earthquake, revealing Hades below and the heavens above. It is the point between birth and death, between the freedom and fear of separation from the body.

Similar to its use by Shamans in Amazonia, the proving of Nicotiana rustica revealed the experience of a journey of learning, of looking at the 'universe', seeking knowledge of other worlds. Similar to the other Solanaceae, it shares the darkness, the shadow side of the world. Themes of black and dark were seen in the proving, as well as themes of light. Several provers had experiences reflecting this broader dark/light nature of Solanaceae; one drawn into mental musings about the "shadow side of the world, no light without shadows, and no sense of shadow without light," another dreaming of "two women, one darker, one lighter in coloring, one character becomes evil and menacing, then changes again to good. She is frightened by the changes, by the oncoming dark side."

Honoring its dark side, many North American Indian tribes used Tobacco as an offering to the Great Spirit, as they would offer the feather of an eagle, the noblest of creatures, but fierce and deadly. Native Americans revered both, and expressed their shared symbolism in the image of the eagle's feather, which they say is divided into two parts, part light, and part dark. This represents daylight and darkness, summer and winter, peace and war, and life and death.

As with other drugs, including the Solanaceae, there is the experience of other worlds, an awareness of the universe outside of the limits of the individual body. This ties into the feelings in the proving of a separation from the body, an immaterial feeling, as if one could slip away, could fall or sink, even into a stone vault into the earth. So there is the feeling of soaring above the world, perceiving the entire universe and then sinking into the middle of the earth, through a crack, created perhaps by an earthquake.

OTHER THEMES OF THE PROVING.

The mental image of the proving revealed a heightened sense of awareness, clarity and lightness, as well as an increased dullness, both consistent with existing knowledge of Tabacum and the effects of tobacco smoking. The clarity and light seemed psychedelic in nature and connected to the feelings of being in-between sleep and waking. The connections between life and death were also seen in the dreams, with themes of birth and death and dreams of the past. The role of tobacco as a facilitator with higher spirits was revealed in dream images, such as seeking for a guide, communing with the divine, and teaching and learning experiences. Both the dreams and waking state revealed a sense of being in-between both states.

Physically, there were strong vertigo symptoms, one prover (#12) experiencing debilitating vertigo for over 4 weeks. There were characteristic headache symptoms, often described as being neuralgic in nature, and also eye and face symptoms which were neuralgic in nature. In the ear and nose symptoms, there was a particular feeling of "openness", which could parallel some of the mental experiences, a sense of opening to other dimensions, or like the earth opening up, creating an abyss or chasm. The nose had some itching and tickling and a delusion of smelling smoke or a herb. The mouth had symptoms of tingling, and a feeling of numbness, showing the alternating state of the remedy.

The stomach and abdomen showed similarities to that of Tabacum, with a sinking feeling, an emptiness and hollowness, along with the characteristic nausea. Along with the sinking feeling, there was a rising feeling, a feeling like a wave, revealing a similar state to the mental experiences of rising and sinking. In the respiratory system, there were some cough symptoms, often of a tickling nature, worse by any cold, air or water. In the chest, provers experienced some sharp, stitching pains, similar to heart symptoms. There were some characteristic symptoms in the back and extremities with aching, burning and stitching sensations. Also in the extremities, there were sensations of weakness, heaviness, fatigue, a sprained feeling, and jerking spasms. All the joints were affected, including the feet and hands. The shoulder and arm symptoms and general aching should be compared with *Lycopersicum* (tomato), another *Solanaceae* remedy. There were some interesting sleep symptoms, especially waking suddenly from sleep, as if from a jolt or a feeling of being half-awake or half-asleep. There was extreme tiredness, even a feeling of complete collapse. Similar to Tabacum, there was an extreme feeling of chill, going through the whole body, including the bones. The coldness was felt both externally and internally. In general, there was a feeling of weariness, heaviness and exhaustion as well as the opposite feeling of energy circulating the body, as if to take off, to fly. There was an up and down feeling, a rocking sensation and vibrations throughout the body, a nervous excitation and pulsating in the body. There was a desire for salty food, sweets and ice cream and an increased thirst.

TOBACCO AND BIRDS

The proving revealed images of birds, often raptor-like birds. Birds are often said to occupy that in-between place. Not quite of the earth, their reality remains dependent on the earth for food and survival and yet they spend most of their time above it, looking down. They are in that transitional place of reality. Recent bird provings may reveal more of this connection.

The following is taken from the following website: **www.geocites.com/RainForest/Andes/1029/tobaccy.html,** written by Paula Johnstone (Lightening Woman)

The Tobacco Bird

The Humming Bird is the Tobacco Bird. In many Native cultures throughout the Americas, the Hummingbird has traditionally been associated with Tobacco plants as guardians and cultivators, earning them fame throughout the world and honorable names; Tobacco Birds, Medicine Birds, Doctor Birds, Birds of Magic, Rain Makers, LifeGivers, Suncatchers and more.

Wherever Tobacco grows the Hummingbird lives. These birds and the Tobacco plants are so related, that should the Tobacco plant die, so would the Hummingbird or vise versa. (We have already lost the knowledge carried on the wings of the Hummingbirds that are already extinct.) They share a soul with one and other. Both of these Spirit Beings, Tobacco and the Hummingbird, reside from the bottom most tip of South America, up to the State of Alaska and into the Yukon Territory of Canada, covering the entire lengths of North, Central, and South American continents. Many different Tribes have stories that tell how these beautiful birds help in the propagation and aid in the reproduction of Tobacco by transferring the pollen from plant to plant. They will even hunt harmful insects that might destroy the Tobacco plants, thereby acting as protectors of the Tobacco People.

Many tribal stories recount for us, how the Hummingbird helped acquire for us, Tobacco seeds, from men that got greedy and tried to hoard and withhold the Tobacco plant, the plant made so sacred to all the Children of Earth, by their Father, Great Spirit. These evil beings did not want to share the Sacred knowledge they could acquire by using Tobacco in its proper way, with their brothers and sisters. In this way the "greedy beings" tried to make themselves more powerful and wealthier, than others, by with-holding Tobacco. Seeing this the Spirits of Air, Earth and Water, met to decide what should be done. Many attempted to defeat the "evil ones" to bring Tobacco for all to share. Many failed. It was through the cunning and speed of the good-hearted Hummingbird that we have the use of Tobacco today.[4]

Chapter Five

Some Native American Uses of Tobacco and Their Associated Proving Symptoms

SPIRITUAL USES

Communication with the higher spirits

Southwestern Indians smoked to empower prayer, and smoke was blown to bless stone hunting fetishes

Amongst the Fox Indians, the gift of tobacco was made by the Great Manitou to offset the brutal fact of the short lifespan of human beings. With tobacco, Fox tribes people could obtain special blessings from the spirit world. When the Creator passed the sacred plant to the neighboring Menominee tribe, it is said, "they liked it so much that they wanted more and more, and he made them dance before he would give it to them." Their Tobacco Dance pleased the Creator, and established this plant as a bonding medium between them and their gods.

As an offering, however, tobacco did not need to be smoked to be efficacious. Early French missionaries among the Hurons noticed the Indians throwing tobacco on the fire before speaking to the spirits. Today tobacco is tightly wrapped in tiny red cloth pouches and left to hang as offerings at sacred sites such as Bear Butte, South Dakota. Prayers during meetings of the Native American Church are accompanied by the smoking of cigarettes made of loose-cut commercial tobacco wrapped in wetted corn husks.

Dream: I was speaking with Pope John Paul in Rome. I simply asked what I could do for him, how I could help him. He told me many of the priests in the Curia leave paperwork outside their doors, that there was probably much work there I could do.
Now, I've never had the Pope (or my father) in a dream before. My family is all Catholic, and I attended Catholic schooling through high school. But I don't much consider the Pope's presence was very inspiring to me; you could tell he was a beautiful, holy and wise man. I had the sensibility of a religious seeker in this dream, and he was helping me by assigning work. The predominant feel of the dream was that I was seeking.
#15, Day 7

Deanna and the Pope are in my dreams tonight. It's like a weird competition for who can give the best blessing. I see one then the other making motions with their hands, just before I wake up. Deanna seems to be trying harder, smiling more. The pope is more sober, more aloof ... [prover becomes violent in dream]. That's when I see Deanna, her arms in an outward movement from her chest, supplicating, offering her own heart instead, smiling, beaming, beautiful. And then the pope, like her opposite, slowly moving his hands with that incense ball. An inward expression on his face, all decked out in white and gold, mostly gold.
#22, Day 8

Dream: I was in a car approaching a traffic light from a long distance on a long stretch of open highway. There were a lot of cars already stopped at the light and I knew I'd better slow down to stop in time. When I arrived God gave me "The Survival Book for Living Through the Rapture". It was all about being grounded and centered and standing in my own personal truth. I felt at peace and deeply in tune with the message. The book glowed. I felt loving and happy after this dream. The connection with God was such a peaceful feeling, a secure feeling. Almost impossible to describe the calm, inner feeling of unity and peace. (This was a truly remarkable dream and I feel it marks a shift in my life, a deeper sense of connection with my God.)
#19, Day 4

The Cherokees referred to Nicotiana rustica as "father" or "grandfather" and believed it to be the earthly incarnation of deceased souls in heaven.

Had dream last night with my Mom in it, something that rarely if ever happens. Cannot remember substance of dream, however.
#15, Day 6

Dreamed of my father last night. Can't remember much. He was looking for me, and there was a house in a city on a hill ... Now I've never had ... my father in a dream before.
#15, Day 7

Nice calming thoughts of both of my grandmothers that have died.
#9, Day 3

I dreamed that I was trying to arrange to meet people in Grass Valley and to set it up so that I could get a ride there. In real life, Grass Valley is significant to me because my father lives there and my sister lives in the area, and I lived there during my first marriage
#13, Day 23

Dreams: I was at a spa getting this strange hair treatment, my dad, brother and my grandmother was there, telling which treatments to get. While my father brother and grandmother sit watching. This is real strange because I don't talk to my father and my grandmother is dead and how my brother fits into that I don't know.
#17, Day 33

I honestly could hardly bring myself to speak. Finally I stammered and I don't know. I felt more like a kid facing my Dad, or the judge.
#22, Day 3

Dream: My landlady is still there and her husband comes down to get some tool- he's quite the builder and I experience some uneasiness. Almost as I would have as a kid if my dad or older brother with their ever-present threat of violence and humiliation had shown up.
#22, Day 10

TO TRAVEL BETWEEN THIS WORLD AND THE NEXT.

Amongst the Tucano Indians of South America, tobacco is used in a very spiritual sense, being considered food for the soul, also a method to directly contact the spirits. The Tucano use smoking for spiritual purification

The Tucano are famed for their "giant" ritual cigars and use intricately carved cigar holders that look like large tuning forks. They sit upon a ceremonial bench while smoking. "Besides offering comfort and rest, the stool provides the smoking man who occupies it a self- and world-centered space for meditative communication with the metaphysical powers. Thus, tobacco, cigar holder, and ceremonial bench function as complementary means of conveyance to the otherworld".

The Tucano believe that their ancestors live on a different plane of existence that tobacco transports them to. The Tucano inhale tobacco and exhale it, symbolic of allowing it to carry their soul outside of themselves.

Thought of slipping into a fold, like bulldozed earth.
#6, Day 1

Thought: Diving, going horizontal and then jack-knifing down a narrow, long chute, but outdoors, black on both sides, a very long fall.
#6, Day 3

With eyes shut, feels as if I start to sink into and through the sofa on which I am sitting cross-legged, as if I'm about to separate from my body, but feeling is transient. Whatever was leaving returns and again becomes part of the breathing rhythm.
#8, Day 1

It isn't my body, it's the essence of me that is doing this, bobbing about like a helium balloon on a tether, sometimes floating out beyond the surface of my body only to be brought back by the short tether. I go down into and through the mattress and then bounce back.
#8, Day 3

I was feeling the bobbing-out-of-body sensations again, when it began to feel as if a cone of blue energy was rising up from my chest and I was really leaving my body via that route. I couldn't really let go, tensed up, and it came down into me again.
#8, Day 3

My body so at ease some moments I didn't feel quite connected to it, as though I was an "immaterial point of experience", a "black essence" in this room. I was relating to the other sense experiences – mostly sounds – as though they were like me, an immaterial point of momentary existence.
#15, Day 1

I half-gaze out into the full-length world map, and I imagine traveling into that world, as going down the rabbit hole into a blue make-believe world.
#15, Day 1

Had a strange sensation while falling to sleep. Felt nothing—a numbness—in body, like I was separated from it. Envisioned my body was falling into a stone vault in the earth, while my consciousness was stable, watching what was my body descend. I was aware enough, and afraid enough, to wake myself up at that point.
#15, Day 7

Thought of opening up crack in universe, being at vortex of universe
#6, Day 1

Sorcerers use tobacco and ritual cigars to possess and control their enemies.

An image is forming in my mind of what is inside me: a field of dappled yellow green light, like tropical foliage, within which is a murky, dark brown figure. The figure seems to be gradually taking form within me and using me as a vehicle to exert its will. The brown thing might be the gradual organization of my anger into a separate entity or it might be the spirit of the remedy. It is dark, primitive-feeling and immensely strong.
#8, Day 11

As for the healer, tobacco is "the foundation of shamanism which is, in effect, the power to cross between cosmic layers" (Hugh-Jones 1979:231). The shaman's cigar is said to be his 'eye' which he sees the mystical causes of illness:

Meditating before proving, thought of seeing very sharp-clear
#9, Day 1

Sensation of incredible clarity in the head, accompanied with sensation as if streaming light into surroundings
#3, Day 1

Went for a walk. The clarity of the air is almost surreal, and the lacy outline of redwoods against the sky is not exactly changed, but has a green/yellow radiance on the limits of visibility.
#8, Day 1

Shapeshifting

In most, if not all, Tucanoan languages the word for shaman is synonymous with the word for a class of predatory animals including the jaguar (yai). "If one concept cutting across geographic, linguistic, and cultural boundaries among South American Indians can be singled out, it is that of the qualitative identity between jaguars and shamans and accordingly to their interchangeability of form". "A closer affinity between jaguar and shaman is hardly conceivable, and tobacco, like other mind-altering drugs, is an important agent of the jaguar shaman transformation complex of South America".[1] Other animals are associated with tobacco's powers in North America. Along with Banisteriopsis caapi, Ayahuasca which induces visions filled with jaguars and anacondas, tobacco is used to transform the shaman into a were-animal to seek out food, healing plants, or perform sorcery on enemies.

When the lecture began I caught sight of the director's face and was quite startled. He had taken the remedy at the same time as the provers and to my eyes his face looked totally changed, as if it had shifted in the direction of a bird—a bird of prey. I actually felt a raptor vibration coming from him rather than a human one.
#8, Day 7

SOCIAL USES

Aphrodisiac

In the Southeast, tribal folklore stressed the connection between tobacco and human fertility/sexuality. According to oral tradition, the first tobacco plant was discovered growing on ground where a man and woman had had sexual intercourse. After finding this plant and smoking its leaves, an elderly tribesman shared that man's experience. "That's a mighty good thing," his people responded. "We had better take that and smoke it." Thereafter special tobacco plots were cultivated alongside the other crops.

I wanted to have sex. It's unusual for me to have desire that soon because we'd had very satisfying sex just the day before. So we made love and the climax had an unusual sensation. More of a feeling of satisfying an intense itch than is normal for me. Enjoyable, though.
#13, Day 1

Tingling feeling like after you've had sex. This feels great!
#17, Day 5

Dream: I was showing my wife's house for sale, it had three swimming pools and one of the neighbors was interested. I cleaned it up so it would show well. Then my wife was there and we started to get sexual in a carport, sort of outside and a friend of hers dropped by to look at a car her neighbor had for sale and she had told her friend about it. Then I woke up.
#14, Day 2

Dream: Having sex with David but woke knowing it wouldn't feel good. In part of the dream there was a young girl in the house and I was checking to

make sure she wasn't in the room while we were having sex.
#6, Day 10

Dream: With my family and brother at someone's house: they all go to sleep and I fool around with Jeff C.
#6, Day 11

Wake at 2:30 a.m. from this dream: In a loft, I am roommates with this lonely guy with no cooking pots. David P. is there and there is sexual tension between us
#6, Day 37

I dreamed I was having sex with a married man. Every so often, I would go to his room and have sex with him. His wife didn't seem to care. Then one time I'm having sex with him and I think "Why am I doing this? I don't even like him."
#13, Day 38

Dream: my boyfriend and a close friend (a woman, who was my lover briefly before I came out 13 years ago) were very interested in having me circumcised. Both of them were examining my penis and trying to convince me that it would look better if I had it circumcised. I awoke from dream before there was an "outcome". After waking, the dream occurred strange to me from the standpoint that I am already, and was in the dream also, circumcised. The emotional pitch of the dream was neutral – I was in control; there were no fears for me; I was flattered by their interest in my penis; and it was all rather matter-of-fact.
#15, Day 6

Dream: A handsome doctor & I are looking for a room in a hospital to have a trist.
#5, Day 7

Dream: I am walking to my car. I see a stout dark man smoking. I try to let him go by first, but he slows down. He tries to stop me & grabs me. I try several times to yell for help but even with significant straining, I'm barely audible. He takes me prisoner in a bedroom where he forces himself on me. I become sexually excited & he starts to penetrate me.
#5, Day 1

Friendship

The Southeastern Plains Indians used elaborate smoking rituals using the "calumet" pipe to seal friendship or trade (supplying the name "peace pipe") as well as declare war, assure safe passage, greet strangers, and make appeals to the deities. Tobacco smoke was inhaled and exhaled like breath, and was therefore a fundamental symbol of speech, or communication.

Most Indian peoples felt that smoking together helped to create a spirit of congeniality and cooperation. "See our smoke has now filled the room," said a Delaware Indian from Oklahoma named Jesse Moses to the anthropologist Frank Speck. "First it was in streaks and your smoke and my smoke moved about that way, but now it is all mixed up into one. That is like our minds and spirit too, when we must talk. We are now ready, for we will understand one another better."

Dreams: being with friends from high school I haven't thought of in many years. Friends who I had forgotten about. They were here with me in San Francisco, on the streets, going into stores. Very pleasant feeling to be in their company once more.
#15, Day 3

After talking with my sister Rosie, I called an old high school friend that I hadn't seen in years. She said that I was lost, but needed to register at classmates.com for our 20-year reunion.
#9, Day 3

Met friends, one of them was having a birthday. They were smoking pot and cigarettes; I got a slight contact high. Then we had Mexican food: I had a beer. Later long conversation with Johnny about his family; felt like I was seeing him, appreciated his opening up to me ... Felt mellow the whole time with Johnny and Cedar, not un-social as I often do.
#6, Day 1

Went to see a friend give her last poetry reading. She is dying of cancer of the brain and spine. She was brought in by an ambulance and read lying down in a bed. Throughout the reading my lower back/cervical area got sorer and sorer. I did sit at the computer much of the day, but left the reading thinking, "What if we could all take away a bit of her pain?"
#6, Day 7

I dreamed of a community gathering at Beaver Point Hall. All the friends our age were there for a potluck and carol sing. [Prover feels foolish but sings.] It meant enough to me to be a part of this community that I would do it. When I was done singing, the party got started. People came down the stairs, lots of whom I know and we had a feast. I think it was Christmas. Then I felt the warm embrace of the community. The anonymity of acceptance, not the notoriety of standing alone. This is a feeling I have longed for more and more recently. When I was younger, I would always do the oddball thing which would make me stand out. Make a spectacle of myself. How I would like to put that energy into something positive for my family. My BIG family. BP Hall represents the people in my community who share my values.
#22, Day 10

Speaking openly & honestly to my husband about his dad.
#5, Day 13

Dream: of going to a party and dancing with friends, talking and having a good time like the good old time out with the girls. That is all that I can remember. Just a nice fun dream
#17, Day 16

MEDICINAL USES

To kill the pain of earache smoke is blown into the inflamed ear.

Burning sensation, redness and pressure in left ear like I'm on an airplane, extends along left jawline, teeth hurt, jaw cracking
#3, Day 2

Pain at bottom of mastoid bone as I close jaw, pressure in ear.
#3, Day 9

Both inner ears hurt as well [with jaw pain] as from a strong infection. Not separate pains but all part of the same crushing pressure.
#8, Day 19

Ears hurting all day.
#13, Day 26

Toothache—a wad of tobacco was placed against. the gums, producing tingling and numbness.

Throbbing pain in tooth, upper right molar
#3, Day 1

Pain right rear molars
#3, Day 1

Teeth hurt, jaw cracking
#3, Day 2

Dull pain in front teeth, extends along left jawline
#3, Day 14

For hemorrhoids, a wet tobacco leaf applied to them brings relief.

Have hemorrhoids with a large polyp
#6, Day 9

Hemorrhoid is very bad. Painful polyp the diameter of my pinkie on left side of anus.
#6, Day 12

Crushed leaves were made into poultices to alleviate rheumatic pain, swellings, eczema and other skin eruptions.

Several small red surface pimples when I looked in the mirror: one on my left collarbone, one on left forearm, left cheekbone and two on back at dorsal level just to left of spine. They itch off and on.
#8, Day 2

I have a rash in the middle of my forehead slightly left of center. I think I first noticed it yesterday. This morning it occurred to me that I hadn't been using my usual face soap lately, so maybe I've broken out from not getting my face clean enough. But now I see that these aren't ordinary blemishes. They are a line of small white eruptions and the skin around them is reddish.
#13, Day 20

Breaking out with pimples between eye brows on forehead & left side of lip right cheek and left side of neck
#17, Day 7

Breaking out on upper lip-itchy red bump late last night woke up this morning and it had come to a white head
#17, Day 7

Noticed a small red eczema type rash on palm of right hand – the upper right quarter close to middle of palm – along the line/crack were small dark red spots – no pustules – slightly itchy (although I have eczema I have never had an eruption similar to this one)
#21, Day 21

Neuralgia at crest of right shoulder, a/c joint.
#3, Day 1

Neuralgia along lateral side of left calf centered at 4 inches under knee.
#3, Day 1

While driving my right shoulder became suddenly painful and 'poppy' – felt like it could pop out – front muscles and ligaments sore – slightly extending down to upper forearm, (reaching forward, staying still, sudden movement) continued motion
#21, Day 6

Right ankle ached when stretched & extended it.
#5, Day 1

Chewed leaves were applied to cuts to heal them, and also used to counter its effects of snake bites after the poison was sucked out.

Dream: In the back yard at Rustic Dr. and there are copperhead snakes all over the yard. Nobody realizes how dangerous they are. Mom, who is also a

kid, is right on top of one – it is staring her in the eyes, about to strike. I am next to her and slowly coax her away from it, but in so doing back into a huge one. I grab it and stick its teeth in a piece of wood. (I am not at all nervous to touch it.) I go inside, feel a little numb in my left hand. Then I see the cats are around the snake, which still caught by its teeth in the wood. The cats are looking at it, curious. I am afraid and tell everyone to stay away from the snake. Then Selah (my cat) comes inside, twitching and contorted down her spine on her left side. Her hips and arms are sunken below her spine and twitching. I scream, "She needs a remedy!"
#6, Day 18

For people with Asthma, bronchitis, hay fever, whooping cough, the dried, powder root is mixed with boiled water and baking soda. Smoking tobacco was held to cure colds.

Discharge from nose watery
#3, Day 12

Nose stuffed up, whatever side lain on, now right side running; left side thick and stopped.
#6, Day 1

Nose-tissue inside is swelling, esp near the root, as if congested but with no congestion worse on right side, tickle in the back of throat near nose root.
#12, Day 1

Woke with dry throat, congestion. Drank water and began to sneeze. Runny nose made me blow it often, maybe 10 times.
#22, Day 2

As I write this, my nose is running, and I blow it frequently. Mostly this happens in the left sinus and lasts for about 5 hours, until I go outside, which greatly improves my breathing.
#22, Day 5

Mashed root is good on boils and swellings.

Subcostal swelling, right side, from nipple to level of liver
#3, Day 2

Jaw is swollen
#3, Day 3

For treating mouth ulcers and inner swellings, tobacco was smudged or smoked.

I realized that sore in mouth is another canker sore. Unusual to have 2 so close together. That hasn't happened since I was a teenager.
#9, Day 21

Nose-tissue inside is swelling, especially near the root, as if congested but with no congestion worse on right side, [after first dose].
#12, Day 1

Swollen feeling in back of throat
#6, Day 1

Furry, swollen feeling in upper throat
#6, Day 2

In shower looked down and shocked at size of my stomach [abdomen]– I looked pregnant because it was rounded from top of abdomen to the bottom – no feeling of being bloated, no discomfort, no pain or tenderness.
#21, Day 2

The crushed blossoms mixed with mint (for males) or marigold and/or prairie sage (for females) are burned and used as a smudge to counter paralysis. For people that suffer paralysis of facial muscles after a stroke, wash face with tobacco water. The body can also be bathed in tobacco water, to help revitalize after stroke.

Woke late, limbs feel heavy, paralyzed in bed, woke few times in morning but kept sleeping
#6, Day 10

Tobacco tea was drunk to relieve intestinal spasms and lung problems.

Woke [morning], Cramp two inches below belly button, better burping, passing gas. Moves from center to left side.
#6, Day 2

Cramp came and went fast in lower abdomen
#21, Day 1

Sharp pain lower abdomen and umbilicus
#21, Day 7

On waking, I have mild abdominal cramping.
#5, Day 6

[During coughing] the pain shoots downwards and outwards from a central point behind my breastbone and radiates into my lungs. The pain resembles a constriction, as though my lungs were being wrung out.
#22, Day 9

Occasional wheeze in chest, clears with cough.
#5, Day 11

Feel like not breathing deep enough & need to take a deep breath periodically.
#5, Day 20

To treat atrophy of the optic nerve, a tobacco wash was used to bathe the eye several times a day.

Sensation as if I can't see as well as I used to. Not better until I get my constitutional and start taking it on March 13th.
#12, Day 46

For Bell's Palsy or other facial neuralgia, the juice was rubbed along the tracts of the affected nerves.

Dull pain in right jaw / chin (radiates to right back molars)
#3, Day 1

Dull pain in right jaw continues to radiate along jawline to 5th lower tooth from midline (actual tooth is missing).
#3, Day 1

Slight dull neuralgia over right eye, above midline of eyebrow. (right petal of Ajna center)
#3, Day 1

Slight inflammation of left hinge of jaw
#3, Day 2

Morning neuralgia in left TMJ
#3, Day 14

12:45a.m. Sharp shooting pain in right maxilla radiating to right temple lasting a fleeting minute.
#5, Day 13

For users of hard drugs, especially Heroin, LSD, PCP, soaking in a tobacco leaf (tea) bath or soaking the tailbone, helps to rid the body of drug deposits.
To prevent worms in herd animals, a few non-filtered cigarettes can be fed to them weekly.
For a remedy for head lice, a quart of boiling water poured over tobacco and steeped. The resulting tobacco rinse is kept on the head for 15 minutes, washed out, and then repeated seven times.

The following story is taken from the Iroquois Nation. Themes of the proving are interwoven into the story which is part of the mythology of the Iroquois tribes.

The Story of the Creation of Turtle Island

Retold from the tales of The Five Nations of The Haudenosaunnee League

---

In a place lived two Ongwe, a man and a woman of high rank. Now after a while the people came to whisper for it was clear that the woman was with child. At the same time the man became ill. He told the elders that he was going to die, but they did not know what he meant for before then none of the Ongwe had died.

When they asked him what he meant he told them that the life would leave his body and he would become cold and still and they must take his body and put it in a coffin in a high place.

Pregnancy; Polarity of birth and death.

The man died as he had foretold and to the woman was born a daughter who grew quickly and strong. The girl would often go to her father's coffin and talk with his body.

Funerals.

When she was full grown she was told by the body of her father that she must marry. He told her that she was to travel to a far-off place.

Dreams of communication with the dead.

Where there grew the Onodscha Tree, a great tree whose flowers gave off the light that illuminated the world.

Traveling through worlds.

And a perfume which filled the air they breathed.

Streaming light into the surroundings.

In a lodge beside the tree lived a noble chief whose name was, "He who holds up the earth". This was the man that she was to marry.

Nose, illusions of smell, perfumed flowers.

The girl, who was called **Mature Flowers**, made a long and dangerous journey and came to the place where grew the Onodscha Tree, whose flowers gave off the light that illuminated the world and a perfume which filled the air they breathed. Beside the tree was a lodge where lived the noble chief. She told him that she was to marry him. He said nothing but laid a mat out for her at the entrance to his lodge and gave her some corn that she might cook his meal. In time the chief dreamed that he should marry Mature Flowers and when he had eaten the marriage bread he took her into his lodge and embraced her.

To his surprise he found that she was with child.

Sexual dreams.

He felt himself to be deceived and was greatly angered because they had not lain together. But Mature Flowers loved the child that was within her, for though they had not lain together it had been conceived from the potent breath of her lover.

Pregnancy; succeeding generations.

As Mature Flowers grew large with child her husband, the chief, sickened and grew weak. As he lay sick in his lodge the chief had a dream and he held a feast for all the inhabitants of the land so he could tell his dream that it might be fulfilled.

Pregnancy; tobacco smoke as the breath of life and communion.

He had dreamt that the great Onodscha Tree, whose flowers gave off the light that illuminated the world and a perfume which filled the air they breathed, was uprooted and there was a vast chasm of broken earth where it had stood.

Pregnancy again; birth vs. death; psychic dreams.

In his dream he sat with his wife on the very edge of this **vast chasm of broken earth.**

Earthquakes, abysses.

When the people of land had feasted they rose and so that the chief's dream might be fulfilled they uprooted the great Onodscha Tree, whose flowers gave off the light that illuminated the world and a perfume which filled the air they breathed, and where the tree had been there was a **vast chasm of broken earth.**

Standing on the edge of an abyss.

The chief took Mature Flowers, who was a large with child, by the hand and led her to the edge of the vast chasm of broken earth where they sat with their legs dangling over the edge. When they had sat there a while, he said, "Now you will depart from this earth", and he pushed her into the **vast chasm of broken earth.**

The sufferings of the chief now ceased and he rose and returned to his lodge. The inhabitants of the land set up again the Onodscha Tree, whose flowers gave off the light that illuminated the world and a perfume which filled the air they breathed.

Falling into the earth.

As Mature Flowers fell through the air, far below the ducks and water birds floated on the sea.

Bittern looked down and said: "There is a woman rising from below", but Loon looked up and said: "There is a woman falling from above".

Ducks and water birds.

Then Loon led all the birds up into the sky where they caught the woman and lowered her gently to the surface of the sea.

Falling from high up.

All the creatures of the water held a conference

To devise a plan whereby the woman should live. Loon said that all who were able to move in the depths of the water should attempt to find a way. Many of the birds tried but none of them could find a way. Then Muskrat said that he would make the attempt and he dived deep beneath the water, but when Muskrat's body came to the surface he was long dead. The birds examined his body and found in his paws and in his mouth earth brought from the bottom of the sea.

Water images in general: rocking in a boat; ship tipping in head; floating, surging, wavelike.

Community gatherings.

Loon said: "Let someone hold up the earth so that it will make a place for this woman to live".

Turtle said that he would try, and they spread on his back all the earth that Muskrat had brought from the bottom of the sea. After a while the Great Turtle said that he would be able to uphold it and as the earth grew so would he.

Thought: something is falling and I have come to prop it up.

Then the earth grew and the woman lived on it. As she had fallen through the broken earth, she had grabbed a white root of the Onodscha Tree, whose flowers gave off the light that illuminated the world and a perfume which filled the air they breathed. This she planted at the centre of the earth and it grew into a great tree, whose flowers give off the light that illuminates the world and a perfume which fills the air we breathe. In her other hand she held a **tobacco plant** which she also planted. This had been the last **tobacco plant** in the land above and the inhabitants there missed it greatly which is why they are so pleased when men burn it for them and the smoke ascends to the land above.

Thoughts of being at the center of the universe.

Then Mature Flowers gave birth to a daughter who grew quickly and strong. She became a beautiful girl and she wandered all over the new made earth. In a corner of the island there was a tall tree from which fell a strong vine and she loved to swing from it.

When her mother asked why she loved swinging from the vine, she said that when she swung from it she felt as if she was held in a strong embrace.

Sensations/delusions of motion.

The mother said: "My daughter, you are married to Ga-oh The Spirit of The Wind and he will be the father of your children."

Enhanced communication and love.

In due season the girl grew large with child and she heard **two voices speaking within her.** One spoke kind and gentle words but the other was harsh and said he desired to kill his mother.

Spiritual guide.

When her time came she gave birth to the first son and called him Good Spirit, but when the evil one was to be born he pierced her through the armpit and stood upon her dead body.

Delusion of being possessed from within.

Good Spirit helped his grandmother prepare his mother's grave and when they had buried her Grandmother said: "Daughter, you have departed and taken the first path back to the land where I came from. When you reach our homeland make it ready for many will tread the path you have trodden."

Polarity of good and evil.

Good Spirit tended and watered his mother's grave and from the place where she lay sprang up three beautiful

Dreams/thoughts of grandmothers; funerals.

women clothed in the leaves of Bean, Corn, and Squash. These are the Three Sisters and each attends to the welfare of her chosen plant. Grandmother saw the Three Sisters grown from the grave of her daughter that had been tended by Good Spirit, and she was thankful and said: "Hereafter by these things shall we live."

Then the grandmother, Mature Flowers, took Good Spirit around the island and taught him how to make trees and plants. But Evil Mind was jealous and he followed behind making briars and thorns and poisonous plants.

Polarity of good and evil.

Now when Good Spirit was full grown he asked his grandmother about his father and she told him that it was time to seek Ga-oh, The Spirit of The Wind, who was his father. Good Spirit made a great journey and at the end of the world found his father. The Spirit of The Wind asked who sought him and he replied he was Good Spirit the Son of The Spirit of The Wind. Then The Spirit of The Wind said: "A son of mine should overcome me." A great struggle ensued but Good Spirit overcame The Spirit of The Wind who then said: "I am your father; you are my son."

Dreams of fathers and sons, including struggle between them; traveling through worlds; tobacco smoke as breathing spirit.

Then The Spirit of The Wind gave his son four bags that contained all the living things that bless the earth. Good Spirit journeyed home and as he crossed the water the first bag began to move. It moved so violently that he could not hold it, it slipped from his grasp and out of it came all the animals that swim in the water.

Violent motion and earthquakes; Water images; Dreams of animals, birds.

The second bag then began to move and when it slipped from his grasp out of it came all the birds of the air.

Likewise the third bag, from which came the fishes and all the creatures that swim in the sea. He held on to the fourth bag but as he reached his home he could hold it no longer an out of it came all the animals of the land and of the forest.

Dreams of forest, animals.

Now when his grandmother heard this tale she said: "We must call the animals and discover their names and we must treat them so that they will have fat."

She made a pool and filled it with oil and into it went the animals and they became fat. Into the pool went the Bear and the Buffalo, the Elk and the Moose, and the Beaver and many others. Evil Mind watched what was happening and he caused many animals that were not desired to enter the pool. Good Spirit seized these creatures as they left, he stripped them of their fat.

Now Grandmother was tired and she took the path into the sky that her daughter had trodden. Good Spirit went about the earth creating and conserving but everywhere he went Evil Mind followed destroying and poisoning what his brother had done. Eventually Good Spirit used his power to overcome Evil Mind and banished him into the great cave where he abides today and where his voice can be heard giving orders to the evil beings on the earth.

Polarity of emaciation and obesity; good and evil.

Now on the earth there was a giant spirit, the leader of the False Faces. For many years he had followed Good Spirit observing everything he did. One day the giant False Face thought to himself: "Knowing as I do all the ways of Good Spirit, all things in this world are possible for me now. Why if I wanted to I could move those mountains."

Delusion of being controlled by evil thing within.

The giant False Face was determined to have a contest with Good Spirit. As he shouted a challenge to Good Spirit he heard a great trembling and rumbling and as he turned around the mountain roared past him striking his face and twisting his nose most horribly.

Now the spirit with the twisted face realized that he was not alone, that he was part of the Good Spirit as was everything that was created. He told the Good Spirit that he would help the men creatures that Good Spirit was to create. His Orenda would enter the images made from trees and it would drive out all the diseases caused by the many evil False Faces that wandered the earth.

Nose as place of affinity/ susceptibility to Nicotiana.

Then Good Spirit looked around him and he and his creation were lonely. So he took some clay and molded it into the images of men and he spoke to them and they lived.

These men, the first-born of the earth, he taught to hunt and to fish and to cultivate the Three Sisters. He taught them to live together and to treat each other well.

He taught them to use tobacco so that men might speak their words to him when he was gone. When all this was done he followed the sky road trodden by his mother and his grandmother and vanished from the earth.

Enhanced communication and love.

Chapter Six

The Proving

REMEDY SOURCE

The remedy was made by Helios Pharmacy of Tunbridge Wells, England, using a piece of dried leaf of Nicotiana rustica. The substance is freely available and was bought on line at www.mazatecgarden.com. It can be smoked like any other form of tobacco.

PROVING

There were 18 provers, 14 women and 4 men. 12 were from the San Francisco Bay Area, 4 from Southern California (San Diego), and 2 from Vancouver, BC, Canada. There were two placebo provers, one of whom dropped out.

PROVER	SEX	POTENCY	PROVER	SEX	POTENCY
3	Male	12c	14	Male	6c
4	Female	6c	15	Male	6c
5	Female	12c	16	Female	12c
6	Female	30c	17	Female	30c
8	Female	6c	18	Female	6c
9	Female	30c	19	Female	30c
10	Female	12c	21	Female	30c
12	Female	30c	22	Male	12c
13	Female	6c			

THE METHOD OF PROVING AND ANALYSIS

The proving consisted of a single blind study with two placebos used. Potencies used were 6c, 12, and 30c. Provers were instructed to take one single tablet 3 times a day for up to 2 days, but to stop at any point if any effect was noticed. On the day of the proving, all the provers from the San Francisco Bay Area met and took the remedy at the same time. For the next two hours, the group stayed together or took a walk alone. Any conversation was kept to a minimum and provers could not discuss their experiences when taking the remedy. The intention behind this was to create an atmosphere where the consciousness of the substance and of the provers could be elucidated more clearly. When beginning a proving in the midst of daily life, provers can easily miss more nuanced effects, so the environment was controlled to see if a greater level of consciousness could be achieved. Analysis of the proving symptoms showed that a few provers definitely had very immediate effects. This methodology has been one of the more disputed aspects of modern provings, some people feeling that it potentially distorts the authenticity of a proving and leads to false conclusions based on notions of the collective consciousness of the proving process. However, the main intention was to see if more subtle influences of the remedy could be perceived in this way.

About 2 hours prior to the proving commencement, a small earthquake hit the San Francisco Bay Area. Not everybody felt the earthquake yet the proving also reflected its influence. Commentaries and references to the earthquake were included in the proving as seemed appropriate. The possibility that the provers were in fact partially proving "earthquake" is an interesting consideration. Given the notion of the synchronicity of events that seems to surround a proving, some connection between the earthquake and that of the proving might be speculated (or hotly debated depending on your position on these things). The symptoms produced did seem to mingle both influences, with the images of cracks opening up, and the feelings of falling and sinking, at times into the earth and at other times just a falling sensation. However, given the fact that taking the remedy, feeling the earthquake, and experiencing the first symptoms all happened around the same time, references to the earthquake became recorded in the symptoms in the same way as any other phenomenon. It should be noted though that some of these images—the crack opening up in the world, the abyss, the sinking feeling—were also characteristics found in the writings of Native Americans, (see above) especially when Mature Flowers is thrown into the abyss, holding tobacco in her hand! Also, in the case presented, the patient spoke of being on the edge of an abyss. Is this a coincidence or part of the dynamic of the proving? The significance of any phenomenon in a proving has to be connected to its replication in as many places as possible.

At both the place where the provers originally met to take the remedy and six weeks later at the prover's reporting meeting, a large map of the world was on the wall. These maps were commented on by one prover directly, especially in connection to falling into the world and the ideas of the universe which came up.

In analyzing the effects of the proving the only symptoms chosen were ones in which (ideally) there was no ambiguity as to their cause. Only new symptoms not previously experienced were included unless very similar symptoms were experienced by more than one person. So-called cured symptoms were omitted, as were any modified symptoms or old returning symptoms unless replicated by more than one person. It is debatable whether to include a cured symptom within the time frame of the proving, as other remedies might also "cure" a given symptom, making the uniqueness of the effect questionable. In addition, including data outside of strictly new symptoms risks including effects that, instead of reflecting the substance's "primary" action, are mixed with the "secondary" reaction of the person, a situation seen in some provings. Some provings tend to include material that does not belong exclusively to the remedy but also symptoms more intrinsic to the person, perhaps being modified somewhat by the proving action and as such the provings become a mix of the substance action and the inherent qualities of the person. One could say that all proving symptoms result from this mixture, otherwise the remedy would have no effect, but given that the prover is incarnating the spirit of the substance, it is the "essential" (primary) quality of that spirit that is significant, not the extraneous qualities of the prover. This relates to the inclusion of the return of past symptoms or current symptoms that are somewhat changed or altered. Their significance in a proving is relevant to the degree to which other provers had similar experiences and that the different "pattern" due to the remedy influence can be deduced. If only one person experienced this shift, then it is not necessarily a unique quality of the remedy being proved, but more to do with the person doing the proving. Other remedies may have a similar effect.

Many proving substances can produce similar results and therefore many provings give the impression of being rather generalized, vague and difficult to analyze. This effect is further compounded by the blanket inclusion of these remedies in the repertory, where they dominate certain rubrics and are found so often as to be almost redundant. By deciding to include only emphatic symptoms, it is hoped that a clear image of the remedy can be seen and that clinical usage will further develop its picture.

Proving of Nicotiana rustica

My body so at ease, some moments I didn't feel quite connected to it, as though I was an "immaterial point of experience", a "black essence" in this room. I was relating to the other sense experiences – mostly sounds – as though they were like me, an immaterial point of momentary existence. Shadow side of the world. Dappled light and shadows on the plants. No light w/out shadows, and no sense of shadow w/out light. Ying and Yang.

#15, 00:00:00

Mind

THEMES

Separation from body; falling, sinking; other worlds – universe, vaults, earth, space, cracks, earthquakes; half-awake, half-asleep; beauty, light; blackness, darkness; birds; apprehension, insecurity and speediness; mental clarity; well-being, lightness, freedom; sadness, weeping; mental fog, dullness.

SEPARATION FROM THE BODY

Taking first dose –My body so at ease some moments I didn't feel quite connected to it, as though I was an "immaterial point of experience", a "black essence" in this room. I was relating to the other sense experiences – mostly sounds – as though they were like me, an immaterial point of momentary existence.
#15, 00:00:01

Had a strange feeling while falling to sleep. Felt nothing – a numbness – in body, like I was separated from it. Envisioned my body was falling into a stone vault in the earth, while my consciousness was stable, watching what was my body descend. I was aware enough, and afraid enough, to wake myself up at that point.
#15, Day 7

With eyes shut, feels as if I start to sink into and through the sofa on which I am sitting cross-legged, as if I'm about to separate from my body, but feeling is transient. Whatever was leaving returns and again becomes part of the breathing rhythm.
#8, 00:00:12

It isn't my body, it's the essence of me that is doing this, bobbing about like a helium balloon on a tether, sometimes floating out beyond the surface of my body only to be brought back by the short tether. I go down into and through the mattress and then bounce back.
#8, Day 2

I was feeling the bobbing-out-of-body sensations again, when it began to feel as if a cone of blue energy was rising up from my chest and I was really leaving my body via that route. I couldn't really let go, tensed up, and it came down into me again.
#8, Day 3

FALLING, SINKING

Thought of slipping into a fold, like bulldozed earth.
#6, 00:00:30

A waking dream of falling through a horizontal space.
#6, 00:00:30.

Thought: Diving, going horizontal and then jack-knifing down a narrow, long chute, but outdoors, black on both sides, a very long fall.
#6, Day 3

Thought: The walls of a house are falling, shifting. I have come to prop them up.
#6, 0:02:00 to 0:02:45

Dream: Going to visit a property in the UP. Dried up Niagara or some other falls. Coming back this guy puts me on this flying tank. His wife is there too and there is not room for both of us. We fly over the forest and are both falling off.
#6, Day 3

With eyes shut, feels as if I start to sink into and through the sofa on which I am sitting cross-legged.
#8, 00:00:12

I half-gaze out into the full-length world map, and I imagine traveling into that world, as going down the rabbit hole into a blue make-believe world.
#15, 00:00:00

Had a strange sensation while falling to sleep. Felt nothing – a numbness – in body, like I was separated from it. Envisioned my body was falling into a stone vault in the earth, while my consciousness was stable, watching what was my body descend.
#15, Day 7

Dream: I move towards the pick-up truck, between it and the wall. I want to get onto the loading dock. I climb onto a kind of mechanism against the wall, one foot on a steel box, the other on the bumper of the truck, and hoist myself up. I'm at the front of the truck. Something is wrong, the truck is moving. Both the truck and the box my left foot is on are rising. The mechanism is actually a part of a lift. I'm just getting my balance; the panic is abating, when the front of the truck starts to move away from the box, pulling my legs apart. The truck is on a turntable and is beginning to rotate. Now I really do panic, as I start to fall backwards.
#22, Day 5

Dream: We are quite high up. I say we because there are a number of senior women up here as well. I cross the flat parts ok, but I am too frightened to cross the arches. I go down on my hands and knees but when I grasp the bricks the whole arch moves. It has become as wobbly as my legs. I'm very frightened by the heights. It feels like vertigo. I won't cross, I'm too scared.
#22, Day 4

Dream: I stare at a still area of congested water, an iridescent film on top, and much life below. I get lost looking into it. Then I am alone in the cave; I see that the side of the road (path) plunges into an abyss. I slip. There appears to be nothing to grip onto. I reach out anyway and my hand reaches something implanted in the ground but not visible. I hold on with all my might and more. I think I have to hold on until someone can help me. Then I envision myself climbing out but cannot get foothold. A second vision comes into my mind but I cannot imagine doing it, a back flip out. I say I can do it more

or less and then did a perfect back flip up onto the path and began walking toward the mouth of the cave.
#10, Day 23

EARTHQUAKES

Working at the computer, I realized I was dizzy; my head spun standing up. Standing this evening produces a vertigo that seems to rock my whole body like an earthquake.
#8, Day 4

During 2nd meditation, a feeling of being on a wave, undulating sensation – just like earlier earthquake though not as violent. (A mild earthquake occurred just before the provers met together to take the remedy).
#15, 00:03:00

Sat on the bench at the park. I thought it was an earthquake, but the bench was broken. Thought of the earthquake before the proving.
#9, Day 3

Today a second shelf fell. That's 2 shelves in 2 days + the attic door on me the week before. It's a wakeup. Also I thought of the earthquake that happened right before the proving.
#9, Day 23

OTHER WORLDS - UNIVERSE, VAULTS, SPACE, CRACKS

Thought of opening up crack in universe, being at vortex of universe.
#6, 0:00:20

Dream: I was going to take a class on "the universe."
#6, 3:20:00

Thought: What if all the planets were on the end of fishing nets and I was pulling them all in?
#6, 00:02:45

I half-gaze out into the well-length world map, and I imagine traveling into that world, as going down the rabbit hole into a blue make-believe world. A feeling of going into a huge world, coming from outer space.
#15, 00:00:00

Dream: The moon is reflecting the planets, and many other things. It's like a holographic projection onto the surface of the moon. I see all the planets and all their moons, rotating and revolving at their various rates. Of course I recognize Saturn by its rings, but all the planets are there. There are also these three odd structures which look like they were built, sort of like spaceships,

and they look bigger than the planets. Maybe they are just closer.
#22, Day 17

Dream: I was looking down at the Saint-Lawrence Seaway, the Ottawa valley, and the northeastern United States. It looked like my Civilization game, with lots of forest and then these square cities plopped down ... When I was looking down on the continent, the forest was in its autumn colors and I could see the twin spires of cathedrals in the towns or cities I looked upon.
#22, Day 7

Dreamed I was looking down on a terrain of mesas lined up in a row on a fault line. The mesas were called "Californias."
#13, Day 26

Had a strange feeling while falling to sleep.... Envisioned my body was falling into a stone vault in the earth.
 # 15, Day 7

HALF-AWAKE, HALF-ASLEEP, TRANSITIONAL STATES

Went for a walk. The clarity of the air is almost surreal, the sky is not exactly changed, but has a green/yellow radiance on the limits of visibility.
#8, 00:00:55

I lay down and went into a sort of transitional mental state for a while.
#8, Day 2

I went to bed and while just drifting off, seeing green and yellow leaves, the powerful, sultry scent of tropical flowers seemed to come in through the window, something like gardenia and plumeria combined. I thought about this half-asleep and slowly realized it was February and there were no flowers in the garden or anywhere else.
#8, Day 3

I was relating to the other sense experiences – mostly sounds – as though they were like me, an immaterial point of momentary existence. Shadow side of the world. Dappled light and shadows on the plants. No light w/out shadows, and no sense of shadow w/out light. Ying and Yang.
 # 15, 00:00:01

BEAUTY, LIGHT

Sensation of incredible of clarity in the head, accompanied with sensation as if streaming light into surroundings
#3, 00:20:xx

Again, desire to laugh, smile, a lightness and clarity.
#10, 00:00:30

Went for a walk. The clarity of the air is almost surreal, and the lacy outline of redwoods against the sky is not exactly changed, but has a green/yellow radiance on the limits of visibility.
#8, 00:01:55

With eyes closed in the dark, light dappled colors in field of vision, yellow and green.
#8, 01:10:30

Shadow side of the world. Dappled light and shadows on the plants. No light w/out shadows, and no sense of shadow w/out light. Ying and Yang.
#15, 00:00:00

Dream: A play being rehearsed. I see it from all angles. Am able to see each actor entering and exiting. A door, sunlight coming in with actor's entrance. Door remains open with glare of light from outside lighting the stage. The light source reverses, comes from somewhere else. I watch as the actors become shadowy then clear. Two women, one darker, one lighter in coloring. One character becomes evil and menacing, then changes again to good. She is frightened by the changes, by the oncoming dark side. My response within the dream: fear and reassurance repeating and alternating.
#10, Day 5

BLACKNESS, DARKNESS (SEE DREAM IMAGES AND PHYSICALS: BLACK GROWTHS, DISCHARGES)

Thought: Diving, going horizontal and then jack-knifing down a narrow, long chute, but outdoors, black on both sides, a very long fall.
#6, Day 3

My body so at ease, some moments I didn't feel quite connected to it, as though I was an "immaterial point of experience", a "black essence" in this room. I was relating to the other sense experiences – mostly sounds – as though they were like me, an immaterial point of momentary existence. Shadow side of the world. Dappled light and shadows on the plants. No light w/out shadows, and no sense of shadow w/out light. Ying and Yang.
#15, 00:00:00

Dream: I saw little black mice, like embryos almost, being fed to cats.
#21, Day 2

Dream: In my bedroom was a mail slot in the wall. Half a dozen black kitties jumped through it into my room
#19, Day 9

Dreamed of black caterpillars.
#19, Day 15

Dream: We hook up with a couple, a man and a woman. The man is tall and broad with black hair. The woman also has black hair and is beautiful, though I cannot remember her features.
#22, Day 16

Dream: A play being rehearsed. I see it from all angles. Am able to see each actor entering and exiting. A door, sunlight coming in with actor's entrance. Door remains open with glare of light from outside lighting the stage. The light source reverses, comes from somewhere else. I watch as the actors become shadowy then clear. Two women, one darker, one lighter in coloring. One character becomes evil and menacing, then changes again to good. She is frightened by the changes, by the oncoming dark side. My response within the dream: fear and reassurance repeating and alternating.
#10, Day 5

Dream: I am walking to my car. I see a stout dark man smoking. I try to let him go by first, but he slows down. He tries to stop me & grabs me. I scream for help as I see other people walking close by. But they don't hear or see me.
#5, 00:20:45

The brown thing might be the gradual organization of my anger into a separate entity or it might be the spirit of the remedy. It is dark, primitive feeling and immensely strong.
#8, Day 12

BIRDS

Feeling of long nose, beak-like. Air coming through bridge of nose, drew picture of long bill and where holes on water bird's bill are, that is where I feel the air coming through.
#6, 0:00:03

Feeling of having a long neck: from crown of head to collar bones
#6, 0:00:04

Thought: "The birds are not singing, – Singing, singing, singing – They are spacious in you."
#6, 00:02:45

Thought: second-guessing remedy, thinking of totem poles in Pacific Northwest having "long bird snouts," "long necks."
#6, 00:11:06

I heard a few birds outside calling to each other. The sound penetrated me deeply, and I felt abruptly that I transitioned into their world of swift motion, passion and keen life. It felt totally alien from human experience. I was up in the air and swaying leaves with them, could feel the full power of emotion and

meaning in their cries and dance, and felt the keenest love for them, oneness with them and their society.
#8, Day 3

To my eyes his face looked totally changed, as if it had shifted in the direction of bird, a bird of prey. I actually felt a raptor vibration coming from him rather than a human one.
#8, Day 7

Thoughts of birds
#9, 00:00:05

Dream: Vague thoughts from a dream of birds soaring above tall trees.
#9, Day 2

I almost feel that this is a bird of prey remedy and my children are the prey.
#9, Day 8

Thoughts of a bird remedy. The relationship that I have with the kids at this moment seems like a bird.
#9, Day 13

I keep finding that I am using a lot of words I don't usually use. Like flying the coop, flighty, free as a bird, just ducky, flying free.
#17, Day 18

APPREHENSION, INSECURITY, SPEEDINESS

My body feels speedy. I feel racy and anxious.
#19, Day 28

Mind anxious, flustered, difficult to center myself.
#19, Day 2

A sense of dread and not wanting to be involved with responsibilities.
#19, Day 2

Feelings of insecurity. I'm usually very confident, but I feel insecure about myself. Still feel like I am not very evolved.
#9, Day 13

Mind: Heavy-racing, lots to do and not enough time to do it
#17, Day 9

Mild, anxious feeling, kind of a speedy feeling, in chest and heart area, like being on a mild stimulant.
#19, 00:00:20

Again slightly speedy feeling, feel it in chest, heart, and upper limbs, five minutes after third dose.
#19, Day 2

I am talking fast when on the phone with Mary. I feel speedy. I am mopping the floor.
#5, Day 2

I feel industrious, busy, cleaning, cooking. Unusual for this time of day
#5, Day 2

Mind – active, jumping, too agitated to sleep, read.
#10, 00:10:10

Sense of emotional shakiness as if from scare after cigarette (cigarettes normally ameliorate.)
#10, 00:19:17

Entire being is tremulous, overly alert, fear of going to bed/sleep. Smoking more to ease agitation.
#10, Day 2

Thoughts flowing quickly – speed, not thoroughness; one comes up, look at it briefly, it goes and another comes up – rapidly, within seconds. No sense of completed thoughts and no need to.
#10, Day 2

Workday – again, unable or unwilling to take time to write notes – state of agitation. Great desire for coffee, not as stimulant but as a quieting ritual – removal of self from time.
#10, Day 3

Very restless, sleeplessness after 20 hours. = Hyperactivity
#10, Day 29

All sensations very fast and fleeting
#4, 00:10:13

Realize I am going thru emotional cycles very quickly.
#4, Day 5

MENTAL CLARITY

Sensation of incredible clarity in the head, accompanied with sensation as if streaming light into surroundings
#3, 00:00:22

I am feeling clear-headed, confident, a deep sense of satisfaction with myself, my work and my accomplishments, life is good.
#19, 00:14:20

Clear, focused energy. Mind full of thoughts which connect. Able to talk through irritation and to see others as human.
#10, Day 11

Took my test. The test went well. My head is clearer than it has been for days. Another odd thing worth mentioning, my cars left headlight has been out since day 3-4 of the proving. Yesterday, Monday, I noticed that the headlight was working again. The light of my car came on as the fog lifted from my head, odd.
#9, Day 17

I think it's time to go on with my life. I've put some things on hold for a while, some day-to-day living things, like work. Now that I've cleared my head a little, there's room to move.
#22, Day 13

Once again, the weather reflects my mood – such clarity and lightness.
#4, Day 15

Mental clarity. More insights about the way energy flows in relationships. Rearranged the feng-shui at work.
#4, Day 19

I feel aware, sharper, dialed in. Keener, have an edge. Not speedy enough to be threatening or unbalancing. I have been very aware of every detail.
#19, Day 2

WELL-BEING, LIGHTNESS, FREEDOM

Clear & free – I feel freed! Free as a bird, a little flighty, I flew the coop today, went to girl friends and said hey lets go to a movie. We dropped everything and went, something I have never done before. I normally plan things out, been a little more organized today – getting back to normal. People aren't aggravating me.
#17, Day 11

Laughing, joking, feel really good, no worries, no stress, nothing clouding up my mind. Feel great. Having a lot of fun- I needed to do this a long time ago. I didn't realize it was 5:30.
#17, Day 4

Need to smile, want to laugh, sense of glee.
#10, 00:00:02

Again, desire to laugh, smile, a lightness and clarity.
#10, 00:00:30

Could be chatty if I was allowed to talk. Trying to follow physical sensations but feeling too good to pay attention.
#10, 00:00:24

Sense of mental and emotional lightness.
#10, Day 7

Animated, open, at ease in conversation and expression. Sensation of a plug having been removed. No control over output, wanting no control.
#10, Day 20

I'm feeling clear headed, confident, a deep sense of satisfaction with myself, my work, and my accomplishments. Life is good. Emotional and Spiritual wellness. A balanced place within myself. Content.
#19, 00:14:20

Remember drinking a beer at Johnny and Cedar's house earlier, how happy and buoyant I felt.
#6, 00:12:01

While typing notes for supervisor noticed that some of the 1st day's words, images and emotions are very childlike, as if I could see myself as I could have been as a child. Sense of joy at seeing connection and the expression of childhood possibilities.
#10, 01:10:20

Felt happy and relaxed and in tune with the beautiful day. Decided not to take the remedy again [tingling tongue].
#13, 00:04:30

My happy mood from yesterday continues.
#13, 00:21:30

I was also aware of a feeling of happiness that seems to be associated with this remedy. It's a quiet kind of upwelling feeling that starts at the base of the spine and radiates up and out. Sort of like water that spurts up from a fountain, but quiet and contained so that others wouldn't notice it. Both these sensations (happiness and tingling) seem more intense when I'm more introspective, but fade out of awareness when I'm more outward and active.
#13, Day 10

Very, very calm and serene feeling throughout the room—people falling asleep—a peaceful, easy feeling. No physical changes yet for me.
#15, 00:03:00

Felt quite relaxed, cheerful and calm [after first dose]
#21, 00:00:35

Calm, stress free day – felt extremely calm, relaxed and patient, feeling lots of love, affection and appreciation of family
#21, Day 2

Patient, calm and relaxed feeling is persisting.
#21, Day 4

Awoke very refreshed. Accompanied by the thought that I would have a completely relaxing day today – no work, study, and no errand running. Just lie around and do nothing. A rare feeling for me.
#15, Day 15

Felt good when I woke. I smiled. Suddenly I was not apprehensive about the day. I was not in a hurry to get somewhere. I felt an acute awareness of myself in the exact place I was, instead of in constant transition. I felt that my limbs tingled especially because they are so involved in doing, which is what I'm about most of the time. This morning I could be in bed and that was ok. My being was not identified through my action or my inaction, but rather I felt in harmony right there and then.
#22, Day 2

I was an hour late for work and I didn't care. Usually in this case I would be either apologetic or resentful. Here I simply got on with my work.
#22, Day 2

Cheerful, dutiful, accepting of others, sympathetic, fairly calm, industrious, letting things go or rest.
#5, Day 2

SADNESS, WEEPING

Sad and hopeless. Like I was grieving the possibility of love and connection in my life. I cried from my toes. I couldn't stop crying. About two hours I cried. It didn't feel like a cleansing cry. It was hard. I haven't been able to shake that feeling. I feel like it's hopeless for me today.
#16, Day 23

Yoga class is heart-opening poses. Doing this makes me very aware of my sadness about Ann (dying friend.) Participate in class for two hours with this sadness until finally in shivassana I cry uncontrollably. Still crying all the way home. So sad for her.
#6, Day 8

Cried again in therapy and all that evening I'm sad and angry about Ann.
#6, Day 9

I am sitting on the bus crying and I don't know why. I am emotional about something. Feel as if this relates somehow to my teenage years. They were traumatic for me.
#9, Day 8

I have been emotional over my father, who is not dead physically, but he has estranged himself from the family. I thought I had come to grips with his leaving, but I am very emotional.
#9, Day 46

Watching sad movie was overwhelmed with sadness, missing deceased husband, three years almost to the day. Sobbed for 2 hours. Huge sobbing and lots of release. Heart hurt.
#19, Day 15

In the morning I was very sad to leave the kids – I wanted to wake up with them.
#21, Day 6

Thinking sad thoughts and feeling quite tearful
#21, Day 6

My Mum called and said she was quitting her job. I was sitting on the couch crying. Not sure why. When my Mum got home she was crying, she was having pains again like gallstone pain. I made her call her homeopath. I realize she is doing nothing to help herself. I can't do anything. My friend says I am like a cow that wants to give more milk than the baby really wants. Sounds better in Hebrew! I was crying until midnight.
#18, Day 12

(Dream of cat dying), cry in sleep.
#12, Day 25

Weeping – continues for over 1 hour until connection, identifying source – how I approach life
#10, Day 4

In store – tears start flowing with romantic music – difficult to contain tearfulness.
#10, Day 7

MENTAL FOG, DULLNESS

Full-blown sick brain fog
#3, Day 12

Dull, clumsy. Just going through the motions.
#16, Day 5

Having a hard time concentrating. My mind doesn't stay on any one topic for very long.
#16, Day 11

It feels like I'm deadened. I feel dull. Loud noises aggravate.
#16, Day 28

Hard time focusing on anything. Today was a bitch in class I couldn't concentrate. Like I'm in a fog.
#17, Day 8

Concentration terrible.
#18, Day 5

Very absentminded. Went to water and trim the plants at Coldwell Bankers and totally lost track of which rows of desks had been done and which not; had to go back two separate times and test for wet soil to find my place again. Between clients went to Berkeley Hort. for liquid fertilizer and drove three streets past my turn.
#8, Day 3

I am making a lot of writing mistakes. My brain is not working properly.
#9, Day 23

Head feels like cotton candy
#12, 00:02:30

Head feels groggy
#12, 00:08:00

Feels like I can't think. Not better until I get my constitutional and start taking it on March 13th.
#12

DREAMS

THEMES

Half-awake, half-asleep, dimensions between; seeking and communicating with the divine, teaching and learning, beauty; out of body, above the earth, soaring, coming into the earth – vault, grave; other dimensions; birth and death. Dreaming while asleep or half-asleep of the historical past. Dreaming of friends, loved ones and scenes from the personal past not thought of for

many years, including loved ones who had died, and of enhanced communication and closeness. Heightened sexual activity or awareness.

HALF-AWAKE, HALF-ASLEEP, TRANSITIONAL STATES, OTHER DIMENSIONS

In sleep, similar feeling to awake state (out of body, free, traveling above the vast world, coming down into the world), going deep into the earth, detached, out of body, a deep vault, into my grave. Far into the earth (when taking a nap). half-awake and half-asleep. Scary.
#15, Day 2

Dreamt of people I had not seen in years, as if I had been in continuous communication with them (perhaps on another dimension). Feel less attached to things, can let go more easily.
 # 4, Day 11

I was not feeling well, so went upstairs to lie on the floor so I could be in the sun. I felt chilly and tired. A bit later I started to have a dream although I knew I was actually still partially awake. I had a dream my cat died and I started to cry. I was crying in the dream but I was moaning in real life and feeling really sad and upset. I was having these surges of energy that ran through my body and head that felt like electrical surges. It didn't feel good. It was more like radio waves surging through my body, especially into my head. When I actually woke up totally, I thought my cat had died and I felt very down.
 # 12, Day 25

A waking dream of falling through a horizontal space.
#6, 00:00:30.

I wake up with a jolt of adrenaline. I lie there unable to move. Sometimes from these dreams it feels that you either wake or you die, there is such a confrontation of worlds, of powerful primal urges.
#22, Day 17

OUT OF BODY, ABOVE THE EARTH, SOARING, COMING INTO THE EARTH - VAULT, GRAVE

In sleep, similar feeling to awake state (out of body, free, traveling above the vast world, coming down into the world), going deep into the earth, detached, out of body, a deep vault, into my grave. Far into the earth (when taking a nap). half-awake and half-asleep. Scary.
#15, Day 2

Vague thoughts from a dream- birds soaring above tall trees.
#9, Day 1

Dream: I was looking down at the Saint-Lawrence Seaway, the Ottawa valley, and the northeastern United States. It looked like my Civilization game, with lots of forest and then these square cities plopped down.... When I was looking down on the continent, the forest was in its autumn colors and I could see the twin spires of cathedrals in the towns or cities I looked upon.
#22, Day 7

Dreamed I was looking down on a terrain of mesas lined up in a row on a fault line. The mesas were called "Californias."
#13, Day 26

Fell asleep rocking and woke like a bolt of lightning from a dream in which my cat Gemma was sitting on my chest and spoke to me. I could see the words come out of her mouth in a cartoon balloon. I think this remedy has psychic elements.
#8, Day 10

SEEKING, GUIDE FIGURE, COMMUNION WITH THE DIVINE

Dreamed of my father last night. Can't remember much. He was looking for me, and there was a house in a city on a hill. Had a second dream I remember just before waking. I was speaking with Pope John Paul in Rome. He was a younger, more robust and healthy John Paul and he spoke with me in a language that was not English but which I could understand. I simply asked what I could do for him, how I could help him. He told me many of the priests in the Curia leave paperwork outside their doors, that there was probably much work there I could do.
Now, I've never had the Pope (or my father) in a dream before. My family is all Catholic, and I attended Catholic schooling through high school. But I don't much consider the Pope's presence was very inspiring to me; you could tell he was a beautiful, holy and wise man. I had the sensibility of a religious seeker in this dream, and he was helping me by assigning work. The predominant feel of the dream was that I was seeking.
#15, Day 7

Deanna and the Pope are in my dreams tonight. It's like a weird competition for who can give the best blessing. I see one then the other making motions with their hands, just before I wake up. Deanna seems to be trying harder, smiling more. The pope is more sober, more aloof. (In dream prover begins shoving stepdaughter around.) That's when I see Deanna, her arms in an outward movement from her chest, supplicating, offering her own heart instead, smiling, beaming, beautiful. And then the pope, like her opposite, slowly moving his hands with that incense ball. An inward expression on his face, all decked out in white and gold, mostly gold.
#22, Day 8

Dream: I was going to take a class on "the universe."
#6, Day 3

Dream: Discursive, philosophical dreams. Instructional.
#3, 00:09:xx

Dream: There was a volcano and it was filled almost to the rim with molten lava. The lava swirled around and there were lights zigzagging just under the surface. A wise old guru-type man sat on a rock protruding from the lava. He knew the mountain would burst like a pimple. It was a good thing.
#19, Day 2

Dream: I was in a car approaching a traffic light from a long distance on a long stretch of open highway. There were a lot of cars already stopped at the light and I knew I'd better slow down to stop in time. When I arrived God gave me "The Survival Book for Living Through the Rapture". It was all about being grounded and centered and standing in my own personal truth. I felt at peace and deeply in tune with the message. The book glowed. I felt loving and happy after this dream. The connection with God was such a peaceful feeling, a secure feeling. Almost impossible to describe the calm, inner feeling of unity and peace. (This was a truly remarkable dream and I feel it marks a shift in my life, a deeper sense of connection with my God.)
#19, Day 4

TEACHING, LEARNING, EDUCATIONAL ENVIRONMENT

Dream: I was supposed to teach this high school math class. Instead of having people do math problems I told them all to write a story that had math in it. They were excited and wrote good stories; then we started reading them to the class. At this point they became younger kids, so proud of their stories. Then cut to Elizabeth talking about her kids' poetry class and showing me a closet with all their work in it. I was thinking, "This feels kind of good; I could teach again."
#6, 00:20:00

Dream: I was going to take a class on "the universe." First I thought it was taught by Professor Casper (college astronomy teacher) but then I realized it was my high school physics teacher. (Though I've spent a lot of time in school, I don't usually have so many dreams having to do with school or classes.)
#6, Day 4

Dream of being in school taking the review and the answers are just coming to me as I am looking at the questions.
#17, Day 20

Dream: I was supposed to be with L.K. She wanted to meet before class; we did and she wanted to meet students. She walked into their dorm room (which looked like a lecture hall) and started asking questions.
#6, Day 3

Dream: I was in a school, and we were talking about a medications and one of the women stood up and said she had been doing a proving and she thought it was Duck, and started to describe what was going on with her and the proving.
#17, Day 24

Dream: Sitting in class learning remedies. I begin by separating them by lines, organizing them to keep track of differences; it comes to me: I am doing it wrong. They cannot be separated by differences and be understood. (Waking, I want to know why this remedy is full of homeopathy dreams)
#10, Day 30

Had dreams of attending night school.
#4, Day 14

HISTORICAL PAST

7a.m. I have a vision of a knight in armor (I'm half-awake).
#5, Day 5

Dream: Some kind of keelhauling party. I'm being towed behind a ship, an old galleon perhaps, and there are 5 or 6 of us on ropes. It's like a social event. We jockey for position; some of us move forward, or prefer this one or that one's company. There is no horror or impending death; it is our mode of transport. There is more but I do not remember.
#22, Day 9

In the first dream, a group of people from the area was staging a re-enactment of a historic event that had taken place there. As part of the festivities, my husband or boyfriend (not my real-life husband) and I were in a peculiar relay race. The women were to walk across the yard and get a piece of paper and write the names of ancestors on it, then return to their partner and then the men do their part of the race.
#13, Day 9

I dreamed I was in an old-west type of environment. I followed a trail into the town. I had to pass by a band of Indians to get there. I went to a store and bought a Tiffany-type lamp form a woman shopkeeper. But somehow I didn't take my lamp with me. Later, I was traveling with my group down the same trail. We almost turned to go toward the town, but then I realized that the Indians would see us. So we had to go the other way and I had to leave my new lamp behind.
#13, Day 17

PERSONAL PAST, RECONNECTION WITH YOUTH, LOST FRIENDS & LOVED ONES, ENHANCED CLOSENESS

The first dream involved me and a dwarf, like in Lord of the Rings, in an office. I work at this place with a friend from high school.
#22, Day 4

Dream: I am worried about the boss catching me in his flat listening to records with two friends from high school, Adrian and Pat.
#22, Day 4

Dream: We are on Preston St. near the corner of Somerset in Ottawa. I used to transfer from one bus to another on my way to high school. Later I worked at two jobs in that neighborhood.
#22, Day 17

Dream: I was going to take a class on "the universe." First I thought my college astronomy teacher taught it but then I realized it was my high school physics teacher.
#6, Day 4

Dreams: being with friends from high school I haven't thought of in many years. Friends who I had forgotten about. They were here with me in San Francisco, on the streets, going into stores. Very pleasant feeling to be in their company once more.
#15, Day 3

Had dream last night with my Mom in it, something that rarely if ever happens. Cannot remember substance of dream, however.
#15, Day 6

Dreamed of my father last night. Can't remember much. He was looking for me, and there was a house in a city on a hill.... Now, I've never had the Pope (or my father) in a dream before. My family is all Catholic, and I attended Catholic schooling through high school.
#15, Day 7

Dream: I dreamed of my childhood home. It was haunted and I was frightened. I was up for adoption and Mom kept trying to get me back. There was a restaurant in the attic. I felt lost and confused.
#19, Day 8

Dream: In my childhood home again. In my bedroom was a mail slot in the wall. Half a dozen black kitties jumped through it into my room. My stepmother was upstairs visiting with my stepsister who was visiting from out of town
#19, Day 9

Dream: I was at a restaurant with my mom, dad, and other relatives. It was a spaghetti restaurant and the spaghetti was served on huge platters that everyone at the table ate from. My mom and I sat at the counter, my dad at a different table. Mom addressed a question to the restaurant owner and he addressed his response to my uncle across the room.
#19, Day 3

Dream: I'm in the bedroom of my childhood house. A child came in and then left. A man came in and lay down naked on the bed. I was undressed from the waist down. We had sex. I recognized that my (late) husband was at the door. I went after my husband explaining that the other man meant nothing and that I loved my husband. The feeling after this dream is that I'm attempting to convince Loyd of my love after some form of betrayal. I want to redeem myself for the way I felt before he died. I had so much anger and felt a lot of relief when he passed, as well as grief and sorrow. A sexual betrayal in the dream. I felt frustrated and sad when I awoke. Mostly missed my husband.
#19, Day 5

Dream: I had kids that were teenagers. I had a black friend with a gorgeous daughter. Daughter had long legs, large breasts, and a long neck. When we got to the playground, I became Sara. My friends' daughter was my friend now. My teenager friend went to play basketball in high heels. Sara (me) sat down on the curb to watch. Kids playing kick a glass bottle. Bottle shatters. Sara (me) protects herself and friend. The themes of the dream were getting old, and as a teenager getting lost.
#9, Day 7

Dream: Standing, watching a young woman. I am enjoying her age, losing myself in observing her motions, energy. I start repeating to myself, I am old but not feeling so.
#10, Day 21

Dream: Boys against girl's college football. I was playing. I watched a few fraternity guys that I haven't seen in years play. The girls weren't into the game, just the guys.
#9, Day 18

Dream: Two or three dreams of old close friends, whom I don't see anymore in real life, who were very depressed and going to suicide: The first one was about a friend who I rarely see anymore in real life due to a lack of common ground.... The second one was about the very first friend I was really close to in real life that I became estranged with due to certain circumstances. This happened many many years ago.
#21, Day 4

I dreamed that I was trying to arrange to meet people in Grass Valley and to set it up so that I could get a ride there. In real life, Grass Valley is significant to me because my father lives there and my sister lives in the area, and I lived there during my first marriage.
#13, Day 23

Dreams: I was at a spa getting this strange hair treatment; my dad, brother and my grandmother were there, telling which treatments to get while my father brother and grandmother sit watching. This is real strange because I don't talk to my father and my grandmother is dead and how my brother fits into that I don't know.
#17, Day 33

Dream: I'm back in my old family home, where I grew up. Karin and Avalon, my wife and child, are sleeping, but I'm awake. The bed is too small, we can't all fit. There is a lot of noise coming from outside – too much noise, my parents will wake.
#22, Day 5

Woke from a wondrous dream. My childhood friend D. was visiting us; it was so good to see him.
#22, Day 11

I dreamed of a community gathering at Beaver Point Hall. All the friends our age were there for a potluck and carol sing. [Prover feels foolish but sings.] It meant enough to me to be a part of this community that I would do it. When I was done singing, the party got started. People came down the stairs, lots of whom I know and we had a feast. I think it was Christmas. Then I felt the warm embrace of the community. The anonymity of acceptance, not the notoriety of standing alone. This is a feeling I have longed for more and more recently. When I was younger, I would always do the oddball thing which would make me stand out. Make a spectacle of myself. How I would like to put that energy into something positive for my family. My BIG family. BP Hall represents the people in my community who share my values.
#22, Day 10

BIRTH AND DEATH

Dream: hanging out at my home: I had Laney (my dog) and another big dog, the next-door neighbors had tons of small dogs. Two tiny, new little ones are nursing from their goat.
#6, Day 7

Dream: at Jonah's new apartment, reading the baby announcement. There were blue, stained glass panels in it.
#6, Day 15

Dreamed I was at a birth. The child was given to my husband to hold. For a moment, I thought he was given the child because he was the father, and then I realized he was the grandfather.
#13, 00:13:30

Dream: Three midgets appeared at my front door, two men and one woman. The men were mentally retarded and were holding babies. Each man holding one baby (newborn) under their armpits, dangling in front of them. The woman was pregnant and smiling.
#19, Day 23

Dream: going to meet Lewaii (a Husky dog who died earlier this year that I was close to.) I had been chopping onions and the smell on my hands made her cry. I didn't know she was so sensitive to them.
#6, Day 9

Dream that somebody I know in Hawaii dies. Attending the funeral with David, consoling the mother of the boy who's died. He is very popular, and there is that warm feeling of a Hawaiian family at the funeral. Then most people leave and I am left talking to his mother. It is getting dark and he is laid out on a casket about to be lowered into the earth at the end of a road in the cemetery. His mother is telling me about how she has this chance to pursue a Ph.D., and she is thinking about taking it. I am wondering whether it is appropriate for me to be there, since I didn't know him well. I am also feeling glad for this experience of death and funerals because I was not close to him so the pain is not heart-rending. I am able to be close to death in an intimate way without the terrible emotion.
#6, Day 37

Dream: We (Al and I) were supposed to go to a ball game or something when somehow both young and old Al were killed. Both of us (old and young) were grief stricken. I was in shock as well as being mad and resentful of my older self's grief because at least she had him for a lifetime and they were old and retired anyway whereas I never even got to start with him. My life with him was stolen from me just when there was hope and something to look forward to. I had been happy and now it wasn't fair.
#21, Day 2

Two or three dreams of old close friends, whom I don't see anymore in real life, who were very depressed and going to suicide:
#21, Day 4

Dream about friend who died. I remembered it Friday afternoon.
#18, Day 11

Dream of cat dying, cry in sleep.
#12, Day 25

Dream: In a building (as a boarder) with a man. Got told my son had killed himself. Paralysis then kept thinking he is only 15. I knew I had to claim his body. My body kept feeling him as an infant. I had to keep reminding myself he was 15. I kept rocking my arms as if holding a baby. Told someone to cremate him. I held the thermos his ashes were in under my jacket, next to my heart.
#10, Day 11

SEX

Dream: husband and I at a restaurant w/ friends. A friend of his went and got food and came back to the table. I'm at the table; this guy said "oh hang on a minute" and I didn't hear him and ended sitting on his lap. Then he said "just a minute I'll move over," so he moved over and I moved next to him and the next thing I know we didn't have any clothes on. We were having a lot of fun. We were having sex at the table. After I got done I got some tingling and I woke up.
#17, Day 3

Dream: I was showing Maureen's house for sale, it had three swimming pools and one of the neighbors was interested. I cleaned it up so it would show well. Then my wife was there and we started to get sexual in a carport, sort of outside.
#14, Day 2

Dream: Riding on a long bus that takes a circuitous route home at the end of day-care. Geoff is there, lonely as always, but this time I actually have a crush on him and am moving closer to him, marveling that I feel attracted.
#6, Day 9

Dream: Having sex with David but woke knowing it wouldn't feel good. (We did later– pain in vaginal canal.) In part of the dream there was a young girl in the house and I was checking to make sure she wasn't in the room while we were having sex.
#6, Day 10

Dream: With my family and brother at someone's house: they all go to sleep and I fool around with Jeff C.
#6, Day 11

Dream: In a loft, I am roommates with this lonely guy with no cooking pots. David P. is there and there is sexual tension between us.
#6, Day 37

Dreams: About sex. (usually dream about day's events).
#18, Day 5

I dreamed I was having sex with a married man. Every so often, I would go to his room and have sex with him. His wife didn't seem to care. Then one time I'm having sex with him and I think, "Why am I doing this? I don't even like him." So I stop having sex with him and he goes back to having sex with his wife. Then I'm in a throng of people walking on the road. I wave and smile at everyone I know. I want them to like me so they'll invite me to do things with them. Then I'll meet their friends and maybe find someone else to have sex with.
#13, Day 38

Dream: my boyfriend and a close friend, (a woman, who was my lover briefly before I came out 13 years ago) were very interested in having me circumcised. Both of them wanted me to, even though in the dream I did not want to and really didn't have any intention of going through with it. Both of them were examining my penis and trying to convince me that it would look better if I had it circumcised. I awoke from dream before there was an "out-come". After waking, the dream was strange to me from the standpoint that I am already, and was in the dream also, circumcised. I was flattered by their interest in my penis.
#15, Day 6

Introduced to two young men in a band, someone my son admired? I am then sitting on a bench watching something off in the distance. It is now night, then day, alternating. In daylight one young man, long blonde hair comes over to talk, sits next to me, gently puts his hand on my right shoulder, sits down next to me, and puts his arm around me. Gradually we lie down together on the bench. Night comes, day comes again. Very sensual, safe feelings. Accepting of the moment, mentally not intruding with logic. Wake up to see we are in public. Get up, disheveled and begin walking.
#10, Day 30

Dream: The two side branches, seen from below the cut have hollow cores, with these tunnels disappearing into their depths. It's sort of erotic, like a woman seen from behind, on her hands and knees.
#22, Day 6

Erotic dream: At first I am in a bedroom with a woman. She has dark hair and a petite build and seems very familiar. We are very attracted to one another but I am a little nervous. Karin is in the other room and I don't want to wake her up. We fool around and flirt, but when she opens her legs wide and invites me in I cannot go. I don't want to abandon myself to this desire only for Karin to come in and see us in the act.

Then we are outside, Karin and I, in the woods. We get to our cabin in the woods and inside are Chester and Sarah, a couple of acquaintances. I find Sarah very attractive. There are two other people there, and they are watching Hindi movies. There are cushions on the floor and the place looks very warm and inviting. Sarah greets us and she is very inviting. The whole situation is quite erotic, and I'm sure there would be great pleasure but then I awaken. I feel a sense of longing; I miss the physical comfort of a woman.
#22, Day 18

Dream: I am walking to my car. I see a stout dark man smoking. I try to let him go by first, but he slows down. He tries to stop me & grabs me. I scream for help as I see other people walking close by. But they don't hear or see me. I try several times to yell for help but even with significant straining, I'm barely auditable. He takes me prisoner in a bedroom where he forces himself on me. He tells me how his penis is large for his size and how "he" used to have sex with "him", that is, a friend. There are people outside of the bedroom, like in another bed next to ours. I become sexually excited & he starts to penetrate me.
#5, 00:20:45

Dream: I go upstairs & see a bedroom set with an ornate backboard that is partly a large clock. The man who walked in earlier is trying the bed out & is enjoying the experience by rubbing his body on the bed. I join him & fondle his penis which is getting enlarged.
#5, Day 33

Dream: I'm in the bedroom of my childhood house. A man came in and lay down naked on the bed. I was undressed from the waist down. We had sex. I recognized that my (late) husband was at the door. I went after my husband explaining that the other man meant nothing and that I loved my husband.
#19, Day 5

Vertigo

Whole body head rush getting out of bed
#6, 00:22:15

Slight dizzy feeling all day
#6, Day 2

Tired, feeling dizzy and depleted.
#12, Day 25

Next three weeks [day 25-45) constant vertigo
#12, Day 46

Vertigo is very bad [for three weeks], feels like I can't think and there is a blanket covering my head, eyes very sensitive, sensation as if I can't see as well as I used to. Not better until I get my constitutional and start taking it on March 13th.
#12, Day 46

Slightly light headed while cleaning the kitchen for approximately 15 minutes.
#21, 00:00:35

Quick feeling of dizziness when shifting focus suddenly while playing computer game – tired eyes.
#21, 00:10:08

General feeling of lightness, supportedness, especially side body.
#6, 00:11:00

Watching TV, the screen had wavy line and was moving. It made me feel dizzy and I had to sit down.
#9, Day 4

Working at the computer, I realized I was dizzy; my head spun standing up. Standing this evening produces a vertigo that seems to rock my whole body like an earthquake.
#8, Day 4

Feeling slightly dizzy.
#5, Day 20

From that day on, I had constant vertigo. I would get up in the morning and feel OK but then gradually the vertigo would start. It felt as if a ship were inside my head tipping back and forth, as if in a storm. It reminded me of the feeling I had when I was pregnant. The vertigo made me feel disoriented, like I couldn't think clearly. It would make me nauseous and I would want to lie down. I felt better if I was lying down, even though I could still feel the vertigo, it would make the ship stop tipping as much.
#12, Day 46

While still lying in bed sense of floating, maybe more of a surging, as if lying on a raft floating in moving water. If I keep my eyes closed the sensation of rocking and floating becomes more prominent and is pleasant, like the surge in one's veins after a day swimming in the surf.
#8, 00:08:15

Every time I lie down now there's a renewal of the sensation of rocking and floating in place like a boat at mooring. Very pleasant, helps in drifting off.
#8, Day 2

The only physical symptom I have left is the floating, rocking and surging when I am horizontal.
#8, Day 9

Head

Crawling on left upper scalp, yawning.
 # 21, Day 1

Itching at right vertex
#3, 00:00:42

"Skull as is a helmet" with slight formication
#3, 00:00:42

Right scalp itchy, scratched for a moment.
#5, 00:00:27

Occasional itching around scalp
#5, Day 3

Forehead feels like a metal sheet inside, along with renewed sense of being tired, wanting to close eyes and sleep. < movement, < open air.
#15, Day 2

Headache in back of my head
#14, Day 3

Headache left occiput.
#3, Day 12

Huge headache [on waking], forehead to right temple like a migraine. Went back to sleep & when I woke again the headache was a lot better. More like a dull throb, took a hot shower & headache went away
#17, Day 2

Migraine headache started at 6a.m. and I still have it. The pain is throbbing, it generates from the forehead to the right temple, sharp throbbing pain.
#16, Day 10

Headache on parietal & temple areas, aching, better with pressure massage on head.
#5, Day 19

Temporal headache with small veins pulsing > pressure momentarily < inside glare of sunlight from windows.
#10, 00:01:40

Sharp pain cutting through center of forehead. Flashes in and out. Pain in left temple and area above left ear.
#19, Day 10

Neuralgic pain on top right side of my head. Feels as if a knot has developed where the pain is. Feels burning and raw.
#16, Day 30

(After lunch) Pain coming in through left temple/forehead still, now boring through left ear (began before lunch, awareness comes and goes.)
#6, 0:02:00

After chocolate birthday cake slight left-sided headache again.
#6, 0:05:00

Pulse (heartbeat) in center of head.
#3, 00:00:45

Have a dull headache at temples and forehead.
#9, Day 29

Forehead right temple all day dull ache.
#17, Day 3

Sustained headache – rt. temporal – parietal region; behind right eye. Headache persisted all night and into morning. Pain is pressure-like, feels like a sinus headache. Sometimes extends down into right jaw. < on movement, of head and body.
#15, Day 2

Mild headache, coming from left sinus, pain and pressure in frontal left sinus. Beginning to spread to right sinus.
#19, Day 11

Sharp pain cutting through center of head. Flashes in and out. Pain in left temple and area above left ear. Lots of pressure in left frontal sinus. Clear nasal.
#19, Day 12

Pressing pain R. temple then L. temple.
#10, 00:18:45

Headache: pressure, tightness, fullness, shifting sites; base of neck, temples, parietal.
#5, 00:07:25

My head feels slightly full.
#5, Day 5

Running caused headache & increased sensation of head fullness.
#5, Day 5

Drinking hot tea relieved head fullness.
#5, Day 5

Pressing pain at root of nose.
#17, Day 14

Inflamed sinuses, especially right side behind cheeks; pressure not too bad.
#15, Day 2

Sharp pain in left sinus. Left nostril was stopped up when I got up. Pressure in left sinus and behind left eye.
#19, Day 11

Lots of pressure in left frontal sinus.
#19, Day 12

Right forehead feels full.
#5, Day 12

I wake up and have head fullness.
#5, Day 6

Slight dull neuralgia over right eye, above midline of eyebrow.
#3, 00:00:37

When I woke up, my head was turned to one side and I had a pain in my skull. It radiated out from the center of my head until it hit my skull where it would then diffuse itself into the bone. It was throbbing and corresponded to the beat of my heart.
#22, Day 10

Head feels tight & heavy.
#5, 00:00:33

Heaviness on left side of my head.
#5, 00:03:50

After rising and walking, I feel a fullness in the head especially around the nose, forehead, and above eyes, feeling foggy and sleepy, neck feels stiff. Want to sleep.
#12, 00:00:45

I saw a friend and asked him if he had tobacco. He was smoking my old brand and so I rolled a cigarette. I may have smoked one more…driving home, a headache began that stemmed from the back teeth of my upper

jaw. I thought I was just hungry and when I got home I ate, but that didn't really help. The headache was worse.
#22, Day 16

Headache worse with cigarette.
#10, 00:01:50

Sensation as if left hemisphere of brain opens in a lateral direction
#3, 00:00:34

As if right hemisphere opens through vertex
#3, 00:00:34

Right vertex extends to inner ear, sensation as if "ear is opening on an energetic level", which is like formication, more subtle, less annoying and accompanied by sensation of opening of capillaries.
#3, 00:00:08

Tingling, maybe vibrating a better word, from upper lip extending all the way back through head and soft palate. The vibration feels like waves of energy about a second apart, spreads to the angles of my jaw on either side and up through the sinuses. The whole face feels more receptive and open.
#8, 00:00:31

Woke this morning 7:10 a.m. with clear breathing in left sinus. I felt as though I'd taken an anti-histamine, my sinuses were so dry, though only the left was open. There was a slight raw pain at the back of the left sinus, almost in the throat.
#22, Day 2

Eyes

Watery eyes.
#14, 00:00:15

Right upper eyelid (inner) itchy, slightly red, watery, burning slightly while writing this.
#5, Day 2

Eyes watery & slightly burning.
#5, Day 4

Significant left eye tearing.
#5, Day 9

Right eye watery & slightly burning.
#5, Day 12

Burning sensation in eyes.
#10, 00:01:10

Pain in both eyes, entire eye socket and around eye – need to blink to open them – lasted several minutes.
#10, 00:00:57

Pain in eyes and temples. Sensation that pain in temples is pushing eyes outward, bulging them out.
#10, 00:00:58

Drawing pain at the right outer canthus through skull to right vertex.
#3, 00:00:07

Left eye is tearing. Sensation of a needle poking my eye.
#15, Day 9

Eyes stinging with tiredness better by closing eyes.
#21, 00:00:08

Itching of right eyelid
#3, 01:07:55

Left eye itch,
#12, 00:01:00

Eyes itching, burning, especially left
#5, Day 7

Irritation at left canthus for few days, Itchy feeling, like dry and tight, even a bit burning.
#15, Day 6

Significant burning, itching sensation around left eye, esp. canthus. Feels dry, tight.
#15, Day 10

Canthus area of left burning, itching again. Sensation seems to be > after I have had my glasses on and am reading for some time. Especially seem to notice sometimes on MUNI when riding home from work at end of day.
#15, Day 12

Eyes dry, tight.
#15, 01:00:54

Left eye itch,
#12, 00:01:00

Eyes tired, squinty, dry
#17, Day 3

Eyes: Tired, dry, itchy,
#17, Day 10

Tired eyes.
#5, Day 6

My eyes want to shut. They feel dry.
#22, Day 16

Sensation eyes are wide open, alert – wider than normal.
#10, 00:00:23

My left eye is dry, worse in the morning on getting up and worse again in the late evening.
#19, Day 8

Alternating quickly between internal and external; opening eyes to look and shutting them; a spasmodic movement, no even flow between but sudden jumps.
#10, 00:03:18

Right eye had redness veins, redness
#17, Day 2

Bloodshot, right side, left eye fluttering.
#17, Day 15

My right eye got really red and itching and burning. Also, the lid all around my right eye was red and puffy.
#16, Day 3

Right eye still a little bloodshot
#17, Day 3

Both eyes blood shot right side more than left, particles floating around like fibers of strings in both eyes day
#17, Day 10

Blood shot, red in right eye on the inner eye.
#17, Day 24

(Remedy Dose #2) Eyes felt heavy
#5, 00:00:30

Eyes feel heavy [after third dose]
#21, 00:10:02

Bright [light] agg eyes.
#17, Day 17

In sunlight, eyes cannot open; aversion to least direct light; small, black specks before eyes in direct sunlight (lasting several minutes); need to shut eyes or move quickly to shade.
#10, 00:01:15

Sensation eyes have been dilated. – Lasted a few minutes until inside.
#10, 00:01:26

The dark room was easier on my eyes.
#22, Day 18

Eyes: Hurt, feeling like they are swollen. Very sensitive to light, I have been in a dark room all day. Typing this is very aggravated.
#17, Day 9

Eyes very sensitive. Not better until I get my constitutional and start taking it on March 13th.
#12, Day 46

Vision

Along with the vertigo was the sensation that I couldn't see. It was as if my peripheral vision was impaired even though I could tell it was the same as usual. It seemed as if my head were covered by a blanket that was heavy and obscuring my vision when I looked to the side. Eventually, it became only my left eye that I had trouble with. It was like a hat that came down over my head, so close to my eyes that it blocked off some of my vision. It stayed that way for 3 weeks.
#12, Day 46

Sensation as if I can't see as well as I used to. Not better until I get my constitutional and start taking it on March 13th.
#12, Day 46

In my field of vision, as I stare out the window, several of the prints on the wall appear to swing in and out from the wall as if they were attached at top to curtain rods.
#8, 00:00:39.

Acute vision. Staring intently on my bran muffin, husband and dog.
#5, 00:01:13

Clear, intent vision.
#5, 00:07:25

1 p.m. Vibration of the tattoo needle caused visual fuzziness while I was tattooing.
#5, Day 6

Vision: blurry in the morning when I get up, clears up about 5 minutes after I am up.
#17, Day 29

Tinge of headache temples – eyes slightly blurred. Gone in 5 minutes
#10, Day 4

Ear

Upper hard cartilage and rim of left ear is sensitive to the touch > rubbing.
#21, Day 5

Sore spot on my right ear just inside notched part of the earlobe. Tender along the inner edge of the notch. When I lay on my right side, the pressure makes that area hurt. I realize that it has been there for a couple of days.
#13, Day 8

3:30 a.m. - I woke with soreness in my right outer ear – the part on the upper ear that curls over. It was hurting even without me touching it but worse with pressure. Pain in the left inner ear was almost gone
#13, Day 26

Sensitivity on my left ear. It felt hot and burning. Sensitive to touch.
#16, Day 3

Ear pain- felt as if something draining from top of head to right ear. Ear pain came in waves every ten minutes. For an entire day. Still bothering me a little.
#16, Day 28

Burning sensation, redness and pressure in left ear like I'm on an airplane, extends along left jaw line, teeth hurt, jaw cracking
#5, 01:10:12

Inner ear pressure increases
#3, 00:00:08

Ears a little stuffy.
#6, Day 2

Pain at bottom of mastoid bone as I close jaw, pressure in ear.
#3, Day 9

Both inner ears hurt as well [with jaw pain] as from a strong infection. Not separate pains but all part of the same crushing pressure.
#8, Day 19

Ears hurting
#13, Day 26

My left ear is full
#13, Day 31

Ears plugged up.
#12, 00:02:30

My ears are plugged up, like a wax build-up, or water in them.
#22, Day 13

Left ear with some fullness.
#5, Day 5

Sensation as if "ear is opening on an energetic level", which is like formication, more subtle, less annoying and accompanied by sensation of opening of capillaries.
#3, 00:00:08

Hearing

Hearing seems more acute, especially in the higher ranges. The room is full of many sounds but I hear higher tones that I wasn't aware of earlier.
#8, 00:03:50

Everything seems to be louder than normal, aggravated, in your face.
#15, Day 10

[On waking] Left ear is crackling & stopped up
#5, Day 8

7:30 a.m. – Right ear crackles with swallowing.
#5, Day 12

Nose

Feeling of long nose, beak-like. Air coming through bridge of nose, drew picture of long bill and where holes on water bird's bill are, that is where I feel the air coming through
#6, 00:00:03

My sinuses have expanded. They weren't blocked before, but now they're as open and wide as possible.
#8, 00:00:27

"Opening" of both nostrils
#3, 00:00:36

Left nostril opens up when lying on my back.
#5, Day 8

Drawing sensation L nostril through to L occipital.
#10, 00:03:00

Nose-tissue inside is swelling, especially near the root, as if congested but with no congestion worse on right side, [after first dose].
#12, 00:00:30

Slight blood from left nostril when I blew my nose. Mild runny nose.
#19, Day 2

Left nasal congestion worse; slight nasal discharge when blow my nose. Improved with hot bath & hot tea.
#5, Day 7

Nose stuffed up, whatever side lain on, now right side running; left side thick and stopped.
#6, 00:22:15

Woke [morning], left nostril to back of throat plugged
#6, Day 2

Nose congested, left side more
#6, Day 5

As I write this my nose is running, and I blow it frequently. Mostly this happens in the left sinus and lasts for about 5 hours, until I go outside, which greatly improves my breathing.
#22, Day 5

Drinking water immediately elicits a sneeze and my sinuses start flowing – aah! It's good to be back at it. The mucous is clear and yellow, very bright.
#22, Day 8

[On waking] runny nose, clear mucous
#22, Day 11

I am sneezing & have a drippy left nostril. Blowing my nose of clear discharge.
#5, Day 8

[On waking] left nostril burning. Loose pale yellow nasal discharge; nasal congestion, especially left.
#5, Day 9

I wake up; blowing my nose of clear loose discharge; left nostril plugged up most of the time.
#5, Day 11

Runny nose, sneezing.
#6, Day 5

My nose itched.
#17, Day 17

Nose itching, burning.
#5, Day 7

Itching at root of nose, then left side of root of nose (left half of brow chakra)
#3, 00:00:32

Itching sensation inside left nostril, outside wing of nostril.
#3, 00:00:13

Right nostril itches
#3, 00:01:00

Tickling in right nostril, extends to left cheek along rear jaw line.
#3, 00:00:33

Felt a tickle in my nose [after second dose]
#17, 00:07:28

I smell weird, putrid, a smell like mucous, almost like very old, moth bally, like grandma.
#6, Day 8

Went to bed and, while just drifting off, the powerful, sultry scent of tropical flowers seemed to come in through the window, something like gardenia and plumeria combined. I thought about this half asleep and slowly realized that it was February and there were no flowers in the garden or anywhere else.
#8, Day 4

Smelled tropical flowers again last night around 11 p.m.
#8, Day 16

I keep smelling smoke and I am not around any one that smokes.
#17, Day 19

Noticing a strong odor, someone is cooking. Thyme? the herb.
#18, Day 9

Sensitive to smell, could smell everything on snack table mainly chocolate-that will give you a headache, smell was overwhelming.
#17, Day 10

The candles had an overwhelming scent, so much so I ended up with a headache, right sided above right eye brow, instantly got headache.
#17, Day 21

Face

Piercing warm sensation on right lower jaw diagonally through to left nape of neck.
#3, 00:00:24

Face: It has been feeling hot to the touch, like I am running a fever, I have not taken temperature. I can't read the numbers.
#17, Day 9

Right cheek feels warm; it began by feeling pleasantly "fizzy" inside mouth next to that cheek.
#8, 00:00:10

My hands are faintly tingly or fizzy. So is my face from the eyes downward, especially the lips. Whole face feels very slightly warm and tingly, quite pleasant.
#8, 00:00:26

Have the strange sense of air flowing in and out through my skin as well through breathing passages, and I feel the oxygen flowing through the cells of my face. It's increasing steadily; each slight intake of breath feels as if I'm in an oxygen chamber.
#8, 00:00:27

Tingling, vibrating from upper lip extending all the way back through head and soft palate. The vibration feels like waves of energy about a second apart, spreads to the angles of my jaw on either side and up through the sinuses. The whole face feels more receptive and open.
#8, 00:00:31

Stinging line between L temple and end of R. nostril, deadening R. side of nose as if clogged or closed off.
#10, Day 3

When I awoke I had a dry cracking pain in my left sinus, which was much worse when I swallowed. It goes from the back of my sinus, around my upper jaw, to just above my upper left wisdom tooth.
#22, Day 8

Sensation of lower lip tingling and full feeling.
#9, 00:00:05

Dull pain in right jaw / chin (radiates to right back molars)
#3, 00:00:33

Some really frightening pains going on in my face and jaw, crushing, on the left side, and curling from my left cheekbone around under my jaw. It seems to extend inward, crushing on the surface but sharp in the soft throat tissue

under the jaw. There seems to be a tight spasm on the front of my left shoulder joint as well. They came on quickly but not shortly after sunset. Both inner ears hurt as well, as from a strong infection. Not separate pains but all part of the same crushing pressure. This sounds like descriptions of referred pain from heart attacks, which would not surprise me.
#8, Day 18

Slight inflammation of left hinge of jaw.
#3, 00:20:xx

Crunching noise when jaw closed.
#3, Day 8

Slight neuralgia along right jaw line, pops when clenched.
#3, Day 13

Morning neuralgia in left TMJ.
#3, Day 14

Tightness in jaw, gritting teeth.
#17, Day 2

Stiffness of jaw from clenching.
#17, Day 13

Clenching jaw a little bit today, might be because I have been studying
#17, Day 17

Slight pain in inner arch of both eyebrows, sinus?
#6, Day 15

Sinus pressure in cheeks, along crest of cheekbones.
#3, 00:20:xx

New sensation: my face is being pressed all over, especially over my cheekbones and angles of my jaw.
#8, Day 14

The facial pressure is there again and seems to have spread slightly underneath the jaw.
#8, Day 16

Brief, deep, sharp pain passed through left sinus to left of base of nose under left eye. It is a stab feeling, one stab at a time. Real deep stab where nose meets face. However, have had sinus infections in past with similar feeling after bending over, and this time I was sitting up.
#19, 00:07:45

Sharp shooting pain in right maxilla radiating to right temple lasting a fleeting minute.
#5, Day 13

Simultaneous itch at vertex of right ear and right corner of mouth.
#3, 00:00:14

Itch at left corner of mouth.
#3, 00:00:18

Tic under right eye
#3, Day 2

I have a rash in the middle of my forehead slightly left of center. I think I first noticed it yesterday. This morning it occurred to me that I hadn't been using my usual face soap lately so maybe I've broken out from not getting my face clean enough. But now I see that these aren't ordinary blemishes. They are a line of small white eruptions and the skin around them is reddish. They don't itch, and there's no discomfort.
#13, Day 20

Face, eruptions along nose side of cheek down to below nose – spotty rash.
#10, Day 33

Bump on nose between nostrils painful on touch.
#5, Day 12

I have 2 new eruptions, one on the right cheek beside the nostrils and one on the left chin below my mouth. You can still see the others with a magnifying mirror in a good light.
#13, Day 37

Pimple on chin, sore and big. Another on upper lip, very sore, another on middle of left cheek, and another on center of chest. They are red, shiny and sore. And big.
#19, Day 12

Another pimple coming up on right outer tip of eyebrow. Painful to touch.
#19, Day 13

Pimple on lip is tingly.
#19, Day 15

Breaking out with pimples between eye brows on forehead & left side of lip right cheek and left side of neck
#17, Day 8

Breaking out on upper lip-itchy red bump late last night woke up this morning and it had come to a white head
#17, Day 7

Right cheek redness under eye puffy
#17, Day 2

Red blotches on cheeks,
#17, Day 30

[After third dose] flushed. Not better by fresh air
#12, Day 2

Mouth

Saliva in mouth and feeling salivary glands active.
#21, 00:10:08

Saliva in mouth – the sensation is as if it is coming up from my chest, not the actual saliva but just the sensation is.
#21, 00:10:13

Still getting sensation of rushes of saliva – still yawning, worse when writing.
#21, 00:10:22

Salivary glands active – feeling of saliva rushing.
#21, 01:00:28

Sensation of slight tightness in throat, tongue and mouth, lots of sensation in mouth – electric like but not quite.
#21, 01:00:30

Saliva sensation again while relating symptoms to my supervisor – kind of electric like under tongue – reminiscent of taking a dose of LSD.
#21, Day 2

Chancre sore on bottom, left part of tongue – painful to the touch.
#15, Day 22

I realized that sore in mouth is another canker sore. Unusual to have 2 so close together. That hasn't happened since I was a teenager.
#9, Day 23

Blisters on lower gums on left side
#16, Day 3

Greatly diminished sense of taste.
#15, Day 2

Food tastes just so so, no flavor to it.
#17, Day 10

Numb, swollen feeling on tongue, sort of like Novocaine.
#13, 00:00:01

Tingling, tip of tongue felt intense.
#13, Day 9.

Tickling roof of mouth when waking in morning, extending to right ear canal. Tickling changed to tingling. Tongue tingling as well.
#13, Day 15.

Tingling of the tongue.
#14, 00:00:10

Tingling left upper lip.
#5, Day 20

Feeling pleasantly "fizzy" inside mouth next to [right] cheek
#8, 00:00:10

Tingling, maybe vibrating a better word, from upper lip extending all the way back through head and soft palate.
#8, 00:00:31

Flowing tingle over and inside my mouth [after second dose].
#8, Day 2

Continued tingling of the tongue.
#14, 00:07:00

I still had tingling on my tongue and my mouth seems drier than normal.
#14, 00:21:00

Mouth: Dry, like I need to drink more water
#17, Day 6

Thirst: Dry mouth, I keep drinking and I can't seem to get enough water
#17, Day 8

Mouth: dry, drinking doesn't help
#17, Day 10

Great thirst, licking lips. Sucking on lips lightly
#10, 00:00:40

Dryness of mouth
#3, 00:00:18

Lips are drier than normal since taking remedy.
#15, 00:00:00

Dry lips, esp. bottom.
#15, 00:21:10

Throat

Heat and pain in throat
#3, 00:20:xx

Awoke with sore throat
#3, Day 8

Sore throat, left front side
#3, Day 9

Sore throat left side at night
#3, Day 11

Throat sore and feels like sinuses are draining through it. (These sensations in throat gone ten minutes after waking up)
#6, Day 17

Sore throat in a line down pharynx from sinus cavity.
#10, Day 3

Swollen feeling in back of throat.
#6, 0:00:10

Furry, swollen feeling in upper throat.
#6, 00:11:50

Throat somewhat sore.
#13, Day 26

Some resistance when swallowing. Throat feels a bit constricted and tight. It's like I have to make a conscious effort to get past my tongue and down my throat.
#19, 00:01:30

Swallowing a bit difficult. Throat feels constricted, as if tongue were slightly enlarged at base of throat. I have to work to swallow past it. Thirsty right now.
#19, 00:07:40

I wake with a sore throat and a heavy congested head. I think I'm getting a cold.
#22, Day 5

Mild pain left throat radiating to left ear with some fullness.
#5, Day 5

Throat: feels dry.
#17, Day 6

Woke with unbearably dry throat. I got up and drank water. My throat feels like it's made of cardboard.
#22, Day 7

Throat dry and scratchy.
#12, 00:00:45

Back of throat feels scratchy.
#12, Day 2

Scratchy throat, better swallowing.
#6, Day 7

While crying my throat itch clears.
#6, Day 8

Tickle in the back of throat near nose root [after first dose].
#12, 00:00:30

Tickle in throat, coughing helps.
#17, Day 7

Throat tickle.
#5, Day 5

Burning in esophagus/throat.
#6, 1:00:00

Stomach

Empty sensation of my stomach. Sighed. Abdomen felt sunken.
#5, 00:00:20

Hollow sensation in pit of stomach and ascending into chest - relieved when drawing deep breath. Passed after 5 minutes, mild sensation.
#19, 00:00:10

8:30 a.m. – Hollow feeling still in my stomach, a little more pronounced for 10 minutes.
#19, Day 2

9:30 a.m. – Worked out on treadmill for 20 minutes. Afterwards, my consciousness is drawn to my stomach and intestines. A hollow sensation like a cavern with echoes ringing through it.
#19, Day 2

Stomach growling, but not hungry
#17, Day 2

Stomach gassy, tense, tight, anxious in mind.
#19, Day 2

Short sick feeling in tummy – stomach rumbling and gurgling – around umbilicus as are all following symptoms – short feeling of air/gas bubble moving around – slight cramping disappearing quickly
#21, 00:10:08

Stomach hurts, bloated.
#9, Day 6

I wake up & feel tired & dragging. I want to sleep more. I have moderate nausea.
#5, Day 2

Nauseous during dinner – almost lost appetite but not quite – hard time finishing regular amount of food.
#21, Day 2

I felt slightly sick to my stomach – no energy.
#13, Day 4

Shaking, faint feeling, stomach feeling sick.
#18, Day 2

Feel nauseous. I ate rice/peas and Cran-grape juice. Nauseous feeling extends to ears on swallowing, salivary glands.
#9, Day 7

Sick to my stomach, but not enough to throw up
#17, Day 9

Stomach: upset, feeling I am going to be sick, (pretzels helped) drinking 7up ameliorated.
#17, Day 10

Slightly nauseous – queasy feeling
#21, Day 2

Nausea strong with rising sensation; stomach, abdomen full of gas but no eructation.
#10, Day 5

Sensation of wave of movement in stomach extending to left side.
#10, Day 5

I saw a friend and asked him if he had tobacco. He was smoking my old brand and so I rolled a cigarette. I may have smoked one more.... Driving

home I felt nauseous. I thought I was just hungry and when I got home I ate. My nausea got a little better.
#22, Day 16

Queasy, feeling of butterflies, empty feeling; sinking in feeling.
#5, 00:07:15

[On waking] I have moderate nausea.
#5, Day 2

Significant nausea in the morning, relieved after urinating.
#5, Day 26

No appetite, haven't felt hungry but have still eaten.
#17, Day 7

I have not eaten much food, yet I am not really hungry.
#9, Day 9

Haven't really thought about food since the proving began.
#8, Day 3

Gassy stomach, big turkey dinner last night, wine and cake.
#6, Day 15

I have felt pretty bloated – especially after eating. My stomach is pooched out – and it feels like there is gas wanting to escape.
#17, Day 15

I still have no appetite, but I am eating 3 meals a day, I noticed tonight I had a little bit of indigestion, burning in the stomach, seems to bubble up to the upper portion of my stomach
#17, Day 17

Stomach a little acidy, churning
#17, Day 22

My stomach bubbles if feels like it is bubbling up to my throat, almost like what I have eaten want to come out.
#17, Day 17

I burped 3 times while bending over.
#5, Day 6

Abdomen

Empty sensation of my stomach. Sighed. Abdomen felt sunken.
#5, 0.00.20

In shower looked down and shocked at size of my stomach – I looked pregnant because it was rounded from top of abdomen to the bottom – no feeling of being bloated, no discomfort, no pain or tenderness – partner said it was definitely fully rounded but not too much bigger than normal.
#21, Day 3

Abdomen swollen, accumulation of gas, internal hemorrhoids
#10, Day 14

Cramp came and went fast in lower abdomen
#21, 00:10:40

Woke [morning], Cramp two inches below belly button, better burping, passing gas. Moves from center to left side.
#6, Day 2

Cramp still there, milder
#6, Day 3

Lower abdomen cramps – sensation of fullness
#21, Day 7

Sharp pain lower abdomen and umbilicus
#21, Day 7

After I talked with my Mum, I had sharp pain, lower abdomen, until I fell asleep that night. Uncomfortable feeling inside from my chest to my stomach.
#18, Day 12

[On waking] bloated intestines, gas
#22, Day 11

Gas pains worse 3-5p.m.
#17, Day 15

Rectum

Constipation yesterday and today. No bowel movement yesterday, and only scant one today.
#15, Day 8

Bowel movement difficult.
#19, Day 5

Incomplete bowel movement – no urge. Off and on again 2-3 days at a time.
#10, Day 14

Violent itching in anus
#3, 00:01:00

Rectum: itching, gassy
#17, Day 17

Stool

Stool is darker color, not as easy to expel, comes less frequently and is harder and more broken-off than normal for me [symptom enduring after proving].
#15, Day 48

Stool small and hard with lots of straining.
#19, Day 5

Intestinal activity feels like things are moving towards a loose bowel movement.
#19, Day 6

Loose bowel movement: stools, solid w/ gush of water and consistency and texture of liver cleansing debris.
#10, Day 5

Female

I wanted to have sex. It is unusual for me to have a desire that soon because we'd had very satisfying sex just the day before. So we made love and the climax had an unusual sensation. More of a feeling of satisfying an intense itch than is normal for me.
#13, 00:10:10

White, itching, thick leucorrhoea (mid-cycle, not just before period, as it usually is.)
#6, Day 29

Tiny vaginal itching feeling when urinating
#21, 00:20:20

Vaginal discharge – bloody mucous – not a lot. Only after urinating would I see it on the toilet paper
#21, Day 8

Began period, no cramps, no physical indication of period starting. Usually slight backache and some cramps. Blood is red, a little thinner than usual. Flow is not flowing yet, show is spotty and slightly mucusy.
#19, Day 5

Menses flow a little heavier at night, though less than usual. Flow is light during the day. Bright red blood, it is usually darker.
#19, Day 5

Menses began – heavier than it has been in the whole past year.
#21, Day 10

Light spotting from menses again.
#21, Day 13

At various times during the day I had creamy mucous discharge
#21, Day 16

Same as Day Sixteen – copious amounts [of creamy mucous discharge].
#21, Day 17

Period appears after 4 month absence.
#12, Day 6

Cough

Intense cramping cough developed.
#12, Day 6

Shallow cough sensation – need to cough.
#10, 00:00:25

[After waking at night] I was coughing from a tickling in my throat.
#13, Day 7

Rare dry cough from tickle in throat.
#5, Day 10

Cough: croupy and sometimes productive. There is a terrible tickle right at the start of the lungs (higher up on the lungs). It was more frequently on the right side. But it was impossible to not cough.
#16, Day 3

Coughed while swallowing some oatmeal that didn't go down quite right. I coughed several times with a gag on the end of each cough. It's unusual for me to gag when coughing unless I'm sick.
#13, Day 8

Asthmatic cough, hard time catching my breath. Lasted for 2 hours.
#17, Day 2

Dry cough.
#5, 00:01:55

Mild dry coughing spell
#5, 00:07:15

Cough dry, shaking whole body
#17, Day 3

Irritating cough, rapid consecutive from throat mainly – irritation in throat. Sudden start, sudden stop.
#10, Day 3

Cough < cool, cold air. Sensation of cold air in throat to bronchi
#10, Day 3

This cough seizes me in painful wracks. I blow my nose, or drink some water, and it's upon me. My chest seems to cave in, my shoulders hunch forward, I am almost propelled forward.
#22, Day 9

Cough after drinking cold water, cold water agg, like my throat is cold
#17, Day 11

After writing for a while I am coughing. There is a frog in my throat that I can't bring up.
#22, Day 10

Chest

Stabbing pain, upper left breast, under arm region. Intermittent, every 20 seconds or so. Duration about 30 minutes.
#15, 01:06:20

Had chest pain on bus today. Again, drawing pains from upper and lower left breast area moving towards heart. This is becoming a constant symptom, though it is only intermittent and lasts but a second or two.
#15, Day 11

I had throbbing aching of my right breast while driving home, lasting about 5 minutes & again but only briefly for 1 minute 2 hours later.
#5, Day 22

Constriction at base of sternum, relieved by burp.
#6, 00:00:30.

Piercing feeling under right breast, also nipple.
#6, 00:11:25

Felt heart palpitations.
#14, 01:23:00

Chest Sensations: slight burning at chest bilaterally above nipples.
#3, 00:00:11

Burning sensation under left armpit
#3, 00:00:18

Sensation of burning at heart,
#3, 00:00:22

Right after I talked to the supervisor I had this heat in the upper part of my body on the sides where the ribs are.
#18, Day 5

Cold, icy hot sensation on left lateral side of torso under left armpit
#3, 00:00:22

Breathing apparatus opens up – deep relaxed breathing.
#10, 00:00:03

Flowing tingle over and inside my lungs [after second dose].
#8, Day 2

Giddy, tickling sensation around my sternum, lasting 1 minute.
#5, 00:00:12

Chest movement more expansive, chest "butterflies".
#5, 00:07:15

Mild, anxious feeling, kind of a speedy feeling, in chest and heart area, like being on a mild stimulant. I can really feel the pressure from my bra around my chest, it is binding and when I place my attention there the anxiety increases. Still mild though. This lasted until after breakfast, one and a half hours.
#19, 00:00:20

8:22pm almost like I was going to have asthma attack, tightening in chest and asthmatic cough, hard time catching my breath. Coughing ameliorated. Lasted for 2 hours.
#17, Day 2

Alight tightness in chest [after fourth dose]
#21, Day 2

Chest feels tight.
#16, Day 2

Back

Feeling of having a long neck: from crown of head to collar bones, awareness of glands on side of neck. Headache still present.
#6, 00:00:04

Slight dull pain where left shoulder attaches to body.
#9, 00:19:05

Neck feels stiff.
#12, 00:00:45

Aching right mid back while sitting & inactive.
#5, 00:00:22

Upper back & neck aching throughout the day.
#5, Day 5

Upper back pain while standing, burning and aching in scapula, directly between shoulder blades. Intense, severe, brief. Level of 9 on scale of 1-10.
#19, 00:14:20

There is a deep sharp pain behind my right shoulder blade. It aches and upon movement it stabs. I notice it mostly when standing erect with shoulders back.
#19, Day 6

Ache and soreness across shoulders.
#10, Day 7

Wake with stiff, aching upper back T 4 up to C I – remains for 2 hours, moves down spine while remaining at neck. < motion
#10, Day 21

Buzzing sensation at mid-back; tightness and pulling sensation follows.
#10, 00:00:55

Mid left side of back bottom of lung or below, small spot vibratory, focused.
#10, Day 10

Feels like some small animal jumping in a muscle, mid back.
#8, 00:00:21

In hot bath. Bubbles which are internal along spine move up spine to cervical disc. 5.
#10, Day 7

Burning up and down spine.
#10, Day 16

Trembling shoulders, blades up.
#10, Day 15

Tremendous pushing pressure from spine to shoulder blades.
$10, Day 16

Extremities

Lethargy. Legs feel like rubber. Yawning. I don't want to get out of the car or move. Dragging myself upstairs. Tired, sleepy. Legs feel heavy.
#5, 00:03:00

Arms feel weak; want to drop them at my side.
#5, 00:04:20

Left arm is weak.
#10, Day 16

Played basketball after taking first dose, knees felt weak. Couldn't run as fast as usual.
#18, Day 1

Weird sensation in right knee, like pressure. Something heavy, still here. When I walk up the stairs it bothers me.
#18, Day 5

Right knee still painful, last night pressure became pain. Now less than yesterday.
#18, Day 6

Right lower lateral thigh felt cold in localized area.
#5, Day 3

Feet exceedingly cold (warm socks and heavy shoes)
#10, 00:00:10

Much fatigue while walking to MUNI station. Legs feel heavy.
#15, 00:21:10

Ache in thighs as if from strenuous exercise or body ache from fever < walking. Trembling begins in bed but at low level, ache continues through trembling. Moves up to L hip and down to L knee.
#10, 00:11:30

Pulsation begins in right biceps, shoulder ache extending upward to right side of neck. Weakness in right hand from shoulder aching pain that has remained for ½ hour.
#10, 00:18:57

Arm stretching, pulling pain extends to interior right side radius
#10, 00:19:37

6 a.m. My left 4th & 5th fingers are numb for 2 minutes.
#5, 04:xx: xx

Right foot pain now being felt predominantly in toe, the sensation being almost as if sprained.
#15, Day 3

Standing on right foot, ankle hurts – pain radiates to foot. Pain as if sprained.
#10, Day 3

Off and on again ankle toe injury symptoms.
#10, Day 6

Right ankle ached when stretched & extended it.
#5, 00:00: 23

Ankles, knees ache, worse going downstairs.
#18, Day 10

There seems to be a tight, spasm point on the front of my left shoulder joint [with jaw pain].
#8, Day 19

Very big jerking spasms from right side. Right shoulder flies upward; hip, leg, knee fling upward; rapid succession of jerking spasms. Releases a laugh – at visualizing and from a freeing sensation; sensation of body being looser – looser jerking spasms – freer flowing than ever before
#10, Day 2

Spasm extends to right foot, now alternating sides as I roll over. Whatever side I am not lying on jerks and spasms. L side tighter movement than right side
#10, Day 2

While driving my right shoulder suddenly painful and poppy – felt like it could pop out – front muscles and ligaments sore – slightly extending down to upper forearm < reaching forward, staying still, sudden movement > continued motion.
#21, Day 6

Bumps with no color, rather wart-like, appeared on right elbow – itchy.
#21, Day 28

On right hand, middle finger, 2nd knuckle, two red bumps have risen. The skin is shiny and very red and itches like crazy. When I scratch it if feels as if something is there, like cactus. I have scratched it raw, and there is a small ulcer there now. It resembles a small blister. It no longer itches after all that scratching.
#19, Day 5

The skin on back of right hand is itchy and looking dry. Scratching felt good but didn't take it away.
#19, Day 5

Large red bump on first knuckle of index finger of right hand. Very itchy. Has a hole in the center, hard, itchy and red.
#19, Day 15

Noticed a small red eczema type rash on palm of right hand – the upper right quarter close to middle of palm – along the line/crack were small dark red spots – no pustules – slightly itchy (– although I have eczema I have never had an eruption similar to this one)
#21, Day 21

More red spots on palm extending down crack/line towards base of thumb and palm
#21, Day 31

Palm still itchy
#21, Day 22

Itching sensation in left wrist, medial side of upper forearm.
#3, 00:00:16

Itching 3rd joint of right index finger; throbbing at underside of 1st joint of big toe.
#3, 00:00:44

Knees, legs feel stiff, especially in the hips, itch on right ankle.
#12, 00:03:30

Trembling shoulders, blades up.
#10, Day 15

Barely noticeable sensation throughout limbs of shakiness.
#19, 00:01:00

I can feel the slight tremors in my limbs and a mild reminiscence in my chest of the speedy feeling.
#19, Day 2

Most of the speedy feeling is gone, just a faint trace in my upper limbs and hands and fingers, a barely there tremble.
#19, Day 3

Woke up with tingling hands 5:50 a.m.
#8, Day 3

There was a tingling in my body, stronger in the limbs, a slight pulsating.
#22, Day 2

Sensation of tingling down both legs as if the stinging, pulsating in back for past 2½ hours is spreading downward.
#10, Day 3

Right palm (eczema spot) burns, concomitant welling up of tears
#10, 00:00:05

Burning and stinging on R. palm
#10, 00:02:25

Right palm stinging diagonally across entire palm
#10, Day 4

Sensation of burning, right elbow medial side
#3, 00:00:22

Burning sensation in left shoulder
#3, 00:00:39

Felt like something bit my toe and there was no mark and nothing was in my shoe. Felt like a pin prick, sharp and quick (1st pellet)
#17, 00:00:03

Sleep

In sleep, similar feeling to awake state (out of body, free, traveling above the vast world, coming down into the world), going deep into the earth, detached, out of body, a deep vault, into my grave. Far into the earth (when taking a nap). half-awake and half-asleep. Scary.
#15, Day 2

Half-awake and half-asleep, (waking dream).
#8, Day 2

Awoke to alarm (for partner, Rod). Strong sensation in whole of body that wanted to return to sleep. Very fatigued! Usually I get up between 6:00-6:30 each morning. This morning I had to make myself arise @7:30 a.m.
#15, 00:19:05

Heavy nap from 10:30 a.m.-12:30 p.m. today after rising at 6:00 a.m. Had very heavy feeling of sleepiness. Head hit pillow and I was right off to sleep in a way that never happens at night.
#6, Day 15

Incredibly sleepy, I want to nap [at 2 p.m.].
#6, Day 2

1:10 p.m. Noticed that I'm tired and could take a nap, not like me to take a nap in the after noon. (After 1st pellet)
#17, 00:07:10

Feeling foggy and sleepy, want to sleep.
#12, 00:00:45

Very sleepy, hard to stay awake, [after second dose]
#12, 00:08:00

Yawning and suddenly feeling quite tired – eyes feel heavy [after third dose]
#21, 00:10:02

Yawning.
#21, Day 2

Lay down for a moment in kid's tent while playing and suddenly very tired – didn't want to get up – just wanted to go to sleep right there
#21, Day 2

Complete collapse – need to sleep.
#10, Day 3

8:00 a.m. – I wake up & feel tired & dragging. I want to sleep more.
#5, Day 2

7:30 a.m. – I wake up but I want to stay in bed
#5, Day 3

8:30 a.m. – Went back to bed & slept for 3 hours.
#5, Day 12

Woke 3 a.m.
#6, Day 2

Took aspirin [for headache], ate at 2:00 a.m. and wrote until 4:00 a.m. (All of this waking in the middle of the night is not habitual for me. After I lost the pregnancies, I began having trouble getting to sleep some nights, but usually sleeping through the night once I feel asleep. It seems like waking in the middle of the night started with the proving.)
#6, Day 19

Woke at 3 again, and then woke a bit before 6.
#8, Day 3

2:30 a.m. – Woke up with tongue tingling, was awake about an hour and a half.

#13, Day 14

3:30 a.m. – Woke up.
#13, Day 17

1:00 a.m. – [Woke from dream], I couldn't sleep.
#13, Day 23

3:30 a.m. – I woke.
#13, Day 25

Very restless, sleeplessness after 20 hours. = Hyperactivity
#10, Day 29

Waked like a bolt of lightning from a dream.
#8, Day 11

I wake up with a jolt. I can't move. I'm not really awake. The jolt pulls me from the horror [of the dream], but I have to make the decision to awaken – I do.
#22, Day 17

Startled awake from unremembered dream – gasping with fright or a scared sensation.
#10, 00:18:44

I wake up startled and dazed, remembering nothing of any dream, became agitated enough to get up too early. On standing up, all dreams returned.
#10, Day 23

Skin

Back of right hand is itchy and dry
#19, 03:03:00

Several small red surface pimples when I looked in the mirror. They itch off and on.
#8, 00:22:50

Mild itching
#5, 00:07:15

Abdomen: itches but nothing visible on skin.
#17, Day 3

Abdomen: cold, itches
#17, Day 20

Itching sensation in left wrist, medial side of upper forearm.
#3, 00:00:16

Feel chilled on the surface of my skin like the warmth is being stripped away.
#4, 00:00:01

Have the strange sense of air flowing in and out through my skin as well through breathing passages, and I feel the oxygen flowing through the cells of my face. It's increasing steadily; each slight intake of breath feels as if I'm in an oxygen chamber.
#8, 00:00:27

I have had a skin tag or warty growth at right inguinal crease for roughly six months (actually, it first surfaced fairly soon after I received dose of my constitutional remedy at 1M potency). Started noticing today that the tag is rising higher, but not growing in any other way. It's a bit sore to the touch also, which has never been the case before.
#15, Day 31

Skin tag at right inguinal crease is still rising higher. It has gotten decidedly more painful to the touch. It is also changing color – the top of it is black, while the base at the skin is red, as if there is blood accumulation there.
#15, Day 34

Chill

Complete and total chill: bones, skin, and organs – shivering with cold.
#10, 00:20:40

Internal & external shivering.
#10, Day 3

Continue to feel chilled as if there is a draft.
#4, Day 1

Chilliness: off and on all day, all over the body, starts from feet and works its way up, alternating w/heat.
#17, Day 10

I have been so cold. I can't get warm. I had to get out to get some sun. Told supervisor I actually didn't call her for a while because I was so cold. My hands were freezing, my body is cold.
#19, 00:14:20

Chill went through my whole body from toes to head went out through the top of my head.
#19, Day 31

Chill, Chilliness: upper portion of body chest and upper back, morning and night.
#16, Day 3

Chilliness: some chilliness in upper part of body, long sleeves made it better.
#17, Day 14

Cold all morning
#5, Day 3

11 a.m. felt chilly
#5, Day 8

Generals

I wake up & feel tired & dragging. I want to sleep more. I have moderate nausea.
#5, Day 2

Lay down for a moment in kid's tent while playing and suddenly very tired – didn't want to get up – just wanted to go to sleep right there, slightly nauseous – queasy feeling, and saliva in mouth.
#21, Day 1.

Difficult walking down stairs with headache; sensation entire body is in distress.
#10, 00:18:55

Energy circulating around my body. I felt the rapid circuit it traverses, like an electronic pathway or circulating blood. With eyes closed this sensation is strong enough to rock me like a gyroscope. There's a vibration flowing downward over the backs of my hands and fingers.
#8, 00:00:35

Felt energy in my body, like I was going to take off, fly or something. Used to feel like this when I was meditating but not as strong then.
#18, Day 9

After taking the 2nd dose, surging and rocking, then the circulating vibration of energy, and the flowing tingle over and inside my skin, mouth and lungs. My sinuses expanded to their maximum again and I felt transparent to the flow of oxygen. The rocking and surging isn't my body, it's the essence of me that is doing this, bobbing about like a helium balloon on a tether, sometimes floating out beyond the surface of my body only to be brought back by the short tether.
#8, Day 2

There was a tingling in my body, stronger in the limbs, a slight pulsating.
#22, Day 2

Pleasant throbbing, like riding in a car on rolling hills, my body has that up and down sensation in the blood. (Is this the vital force being called upon?)
#8, 00:11:30

Very aware of my pulse. I can feel it in my eardrums, see it by looking at my wrist, and it seems to shake my body slightly. Heightened by closing my eyes.
#8, 00:22:50

Feeling of pulse reverberating with echoes through whole body while sitting down with legs crossed.
#6, Day 3

Lying on right side: tingling, stinging, and burning on entire left side shoulder down to feet, posterior and anterior. Eases in 15 minutes.
#10, Day 11

Nerve excitation. Concomitant: heat rising from entire body.
#10, Day 15

Strings being pulled slowly through nerves – an exquisite sensation. Pulling away from spine towards left. Then a sensation of unraveling of nerves concomitant with drawing sensation.

#10, Day 16

Much energy at all levels; sensation of being a changed person.
#10, Day 18

Observation: cigarettes slow down the increasing energy - moderates energy.
#10, Day 20

I feel slightly benumbed, not unpleasant
#8, 00:00:39

Sensation that entire torso, neck down, was swollen, obese, rolls of fat layered downward.
#10, 00:02:16

Noticed that I seem to be losing weight.
#8, 02:00:05

Feels like I've dropped 2-3 pounds. I can tell by the way my clothes fit.
#19, Day 3

I also lost ten pounds
#14, Day 36

Lost 3-4 pounds.
#5, Day 11

This morning my daughter got me on the scale. I have gained 10 pounds. I don't know where it came from (yeah right).
#9, Day 22

During this time, I started a new job and lost 25 pounds
#3, Day 24

It's foggy today but not too cold. I notice that the cool damp open air feels good to me when ordinarily I like warm dry air. I remember that I noticed this yesterday as well. It wasn't as foggy then, but it was cool and somewhat humid and felt good.
#13, Day 35

I want it to be sunny, would rather it be sunny.
#19, Day 3

My muscles & mind are relaxed.
#5, 00:01:25

All sensations very fast and fleeting
#21, 00:10:13

Burning pulsations up and down spine. Feel as if I am vibrating but empty – no energy anywhere.
#10, 02:05:00

Tiredness
#3, Day 3

[Awaken] slightly tired.
#3, Day 9

Very tired, feeling like I don't want to get out of bed (unusual for me), Totally tired.
#6, 00:22:15

Very fatigued. [Morning on waking]
#15, 00:19:05

Much fatigue while walking to MUNI station.
#15, 00:21:00

Got busy and symptoms gone but still tired
#21, Day 2

Extremely tired, feel dizzy and depleted. Can't get enough sleep.
#12, Day 25

Left work. Exhausted. I have had enough of physical pain. Don't need this any more.
#10, Day 4

Next three weeks (day 25-45) constant tiredness
#12, Day 46

Lethargy. I don't want to get out of the car or move. Dragging myself upstairs.
#5, 00:03:00

I keep drinking and I can't seem to get enough water
#17, Day 9

Craves water
#3, Day 13

[On waking] thirst.
#22, Day 11

Craving salt, not thirsty- drank hot tea.
#17, Day 5

Craving salt, cold drinks, tired afternoon 3p.m.
#17, Day 10

Memory: turkey, mashed potatoes, gravy, salty and yum. (Salty is not usually especially delicious to me, sweet my usual craving.)
#6, 00:11:50

All week: craves ice cream at night
#3, Day 9

I am craving ice cream. I've had ice cream every day for the last five days and I'm thinking about having more. This is new.
#19, Day 25

Craving more sweets than usual. Feel like I deserve dessert!
#19, Day 5

Craving sweets again, unusual for me.
#19, Day 16

Craving salt, fish, sweets
#17, Day 6

Chapter Seven

Nicotiana Rubrics

The following rubrics are taken from the proving. They are designed to be referenced from this book and as such have been documented exhaustively, including creating some new rubrics as were expressed in the proving. Some repetition in sub-rubrics have therefore been included. Not all these rubrics would necessarily be included in the various repertories as inclusion in the broader rubric may be sufficient without repetition in sub-rubrics. Those symptoms seen in bold are new rubrics, not currently found in the repertories. Those rubrics with the number found after it have been designated a 2nd degree of intensity. All other rubrics will have a single level of intensity. No rubric was given a 3rd level of intensity, requiring clinical verification before being given that level.

MIND

Mind, Absentminded (1 PROVER)
Mind, Alert (6 PROVERS)
Mind, Anxiety (3 PROVERS)
Mind, Anxiety - hurry with (1 PROVER)
Mind, Anxiety - tobacco, from smoking (1 PROVER)
Mind, Anxiety - shuddering, with (1 PROVER)
Mind, Awareness, heightened (1 PROVER)
Mind, Awkward (1 PROVER)

Mind, Buoyancy (4 PROVERS)
Mind, Chaotic (1 PROVER)
Mind, Cheerful (4 PROVERS)
Mind, Clarity of mind (8 PROVERS)
Mind, Concentration - difficult (3 PROVERS)
Mind, Concentration - impossible (1 PROVER)
Mind, Conscientious (1 PROVER)
Mind, Confident (1 PROVER)
Mind, Confusion of mind (4 PROVERS)
Mind, Content (1 PROVER)
Mind, Content - himself with (1 PROVER)
Mind, Content - himself with, world, and the (1 PROVER)
Mind, Delusions, beautiful (1 PROVER)
Mind, Delusions, bird - seeing birds (3 PROVERS)
Mind, Delusions, birds, seeing birds, **of prey** (2 PROVERS)
Mind, Delusions - **birds; bird of prey; seeing a human metamorphose into a** (1 PROVER)
Mind, Delusions - **birds; her children are birds** (1 PROVER)
Mind, Delusions - **birds; remedy is a bird of prey and her children its prey** (1 PROVER)
Mind, Delusions - Black, objects and people, sees (3 PROVERS)
Mind, Delusions - Body, immaterial (1 PROVER)
Mind, Delusions - Body, **sinking** (1 PROVER)
Mind, Delusions - air, flowing through him, is (2 PROVERS)
Mind, Delusions - body, loosening, is, from jerking spasms (1 PROVER)
Mind, Delusions - body, out of the body (4 PROVERS)
Mind, Delusions - body, out of the body; **on short tether like helium balloon** (1 PROVER)
Mind, Delusions - body, out of the body, lying in bed, when (2 PROVERS)
Mind, Delusions - crack in his soul, or in the universe (1 PROVER)
Mind, Delusions - earthquake, one were in a (3 PROVERS)
Mind, Delusions - falling, he is (1 PROVER)
Mind, Delusions - falling, **space from** (1 PROVER)
Mind, Delusions - falling, **stone vault in** (1 PROVER)
Mind, Delusions - falling, walls are (1 PROVER)
Mind, Delusions - floating, air in (1 PROVER)
Mind, Delusions - floating, **balloon, like a** (1 PROVER)
Mind, Delusions, light, dark, and (1 PROVER)
Mind, Delusions - light [= brightness], **streaming from self into surroundings** (1 PROVER)
Mind, Delusions - light [=brightness], **green and yellow dappled, with eyes closed** (1 PROVER)
Mind, Delusions - light, is light, he (=incorporeal) (3 PROVERS)

Mind, Delusions - **man; dark man is inside her** (1 PROVER)
Mind, Delusions - **map is a real world into which he can fall** (1 PROVER)
Mind, Delusions - motion, all parts being in motion (3 PROVERS)
Mind, Delusions - motion, up and down, delusion of a motion (3 PROVERS)
Mind, Delusions - motion, downward (3 PROVERS)
Mind, Delusions - motion, **falling from space into unknown world** (1 PROVER)
Mind, Delusions - motion, **wavelike (rocking, surging)** (3 PROVERS)
Mind, Delusions - **neck, long has** (1 PROVER)
Mind, Delusions - numb, being (1 PROVER)
Mind, Delusions - possessed, being; **by the remedy** (1 PROVER)
Mind, Delusions - possessed, being; **by the personification of her anger** (1 PROVER)
Mind, Delusions - separated - body - mind are separated, body and (2 PROVERS)
Mind, Delusions - sinking, to be (3 PROVERS)
Mind, Delusions - sleep, half-asleep, he were (5 PROVERS)
Mind, Delusions - space, carried into, he was (2 PROVERS)
Mind, Delusions - space, **outer space, being in** (2 PROVERS)
Mind, Delusions - transition, she is in (1 PROVER)
Mind, Delusions - traveling worlds, through (1 PROVER)
Mind, Delusions - **universe, vortex of, being at** (1 PROVER)
Mind, Disconcerted (1 PROVER)
Mind, Dream, as if in a (3 PROVERS)
Mind, Dullness (8 PROVERS)
Mind, Excitement (3 PROVERS)
Mind, Excitement - coffee, **desire for to ameliorate** (1 PROVER)
Mind, Excitement - hurried, as if (1 PROVER)
Mind, Excitement - nervous (3 PROVERS)
Mind, Excitement - smoking amel (1 PROVER)
Mind, Exertion, Aversion (3 PROVERS)
Mind, fear (3 PROVERS)
Mind, fear, falling of (1 PROVER)
Mind, fear, falling of, backward (1 PROVER)
Mind, fear, heights of (1 PROVER)
Mind, Fear - sleep, go to sleep; fear to (1 PROVER)
Mind, Freedom, remarkable (3 PROVERS)
Mind, Harmony - **feeling in harmony with world** (1 PROVER)
Mind, Hurry, haste (1 PROVER)
Mind, Hurry, haste, occupation in (1 PROVER)
Mind, Ideas, abundant (3 PROVERS)
Mind, Impulsive (1 PROVER)
Mind, Industrious, mania for work (1 PROVER)
Mind, Jesting (1 PROVER)
Mind, Joy (2 PROVERS)
Mind, Joy - **sense, in, of her own childlike possibilities** (1 PROVER)

Mind, Laughing (1 PROVER)
Mind, Laughing - desire to laugh (1 PROVER)
Mind, Love - exalted love, family, for her (1 PROVER)
Mind, Mistakes - writing, in (1 PROVER)
Mind, Patience (3 PROVERS)
Mind, Restlessness -move, must constantly (2 PROVERS)
Mind, Sadness (7 PROVERS)
Mind, Sadness - **forsaken feeling, over** (1 PROVER)
Mind, Sadness - grief, after (1 PROVER)
Mind, Sadness - love; from disappointed (1 PROVER)
Mind, Sadness - **parting with loved ones, over** (3 PROVERS)
Mind, Sensitive - Noise, to; loud noise (1 PROVER)
Mind, Sensitive - Odors, to (4 PROVERS)
Mind, Smiling (1 PROVER)
Mind, Speech - fluent (2 PROVERS)
Mind, Speech - hasty (1 PROVER)
Mind, **Speediness - sense of, in mind and body** (6 PROVERS)

Mind, Sympathetic (2 PROVERS)
Mind, Thoughts - birds, of (4 PROVERS)
Mind, Thoughts - birds, of; birds of prey (2 PROVERS)
Mind, Thoughts - dead loves ones, of (3 PROVERS)
Mind, Thoughts - **falling; down a long black chute, of** (1 PROVER)
Mind, Thoughts - **falling; down into a stone vault** (1 PROVER)
Mind, Thoughts - **light and shadow, of** (1 PROVER)
Mind, Thoughts - **momentary existence, of one's own** (1 PROVER)
Mind, Thoughts - **pulling the planets in with a fishing net** (1 PROVER)
Mind, Thoughts - **sinking into the shifting earth** (1 PROVER)
Mind, Thoughts - **universe, crack opening in** (1 PROVER)
Mind, Thoughts - **universe, being at the vortex of** (1 PROVER)
Mind, Thoughts - **Yin and Yang, of** (1 PROVER)
Mind, Thoughts - rapid, quick (2 PROVERS)
Mind, Thoughts - rush, flow of (2 PROVERS)
Mind, **Transitional state - waking and sleeping, between** (3 PROVERS)
Mind, Tranquillity (7 PROVERS)
Mind, Vivacious (1 PROVER)
Mind, Weeping (6 PROVERS)
Mind, Weeping - causeless (1 PROVER)
Mind, Weeping - dreaming, while (1 PROVER)
Mind, Weeping - involuntary (1 PROVER)
Mind, Weeping - music from (1 PROVER)
Mind, Weeping - past events, thinking of (1 PROVER)
Mind, Weeping - sleep, in (1 PROVER)
Mind, Weeping - sobbing; weeping with (1 PROVER)
Mind, **Well-being - sense of** (5 PROVERS)

DREAMS

Dreams, Adoption (1 PROVER)
Dreams, Amorous (4 PROVERS)
Dreams, Animals (6 PROVERS)
Dreams, Animals, black (3 PROVERS)
Dreams, Animals - talking (1 PROVER)
Dreams, Animals - **giving homeopathic treatment to** (1 PROVER)
Dreams, **awake, while** (1 PROVER)
Dreams, Birds (2 PROVERS)
Dreams, Birds, prey of (2 PROVERS)
Dreams, **Black - black caterpillars** (1 PROVER)
Dreams, **Black - black cats** (1 PROVER)
Dreams, **Black - black mice** (1 PROVER)
Dreams, **Black - black haired man and woman** (1 PROVER)
Dreams, **Black, objects** (1 PROVER)
Dreams, Body, **out of** (1 PROVER)
Dreams, Brother (2 PROVERS)
Dreams, Cats (4 PROVERS)
Dream, Cats - **black** (1 PROVER)
Dreams, Childbirth (3 PROVERS)
Dreams, Children, about - newborns (2 PROVERS)
Dreams, Children (3 PROVERS)
Dreams, Children - responsibility for (1 PROVER)
Dreams, **Closeness with friends and loved ones, renewing** (2 PROVERS)
Dreams, **Confrontation of waking and dream worlds** (3 PROVERS)
Dreams, Coition (5 PROVERS)
Dreams, Coition - **public location, in** (2 PROVERS)
Dreams, **Dark man, smoking** (1 PROVER)
Dreams, Darkness (1 PROVER)
Dreams, Dead, of the (4 PROVERS)
Dreams, Death - friend, of a (2 PROVERS)
Dreams, Death - pets; of dead (2 PROVERS)
Dreams, Death - relatives; of (2 PROVERS)
Dreams, Death - relatives; of - husband, of her (1 PROVER)
Dreams, Death - relatives; of - **son, of her** (1 PROVER)
Dreams, Eating - **family and friends, with** (1 PROVER)
Dreams, **Estranged - friends and loved ones, of** (2 PROVERS)
Dreams, Events, past, long (2 PROVERS)
Dreams, Falling (5 PROVERS)
Dreams, Falling - airplane, from (1 PROVER)
Dreams, Falling, abyss, into an (2 PROVERS)
Dreams, Falling, backwards (1 PROVER)
Dreams, Falling - **fear of, in dream** (1 PROVER)
Dreams, Falling - **saving oneself from** (1 PROVER)

Dreams, Falling - **deep into the Earth** (1 PROVER)
Dreams, Falling - grave, into a (1 PROVER)
Dreams, Falling - height, from a (1 PROVER)
Dreams, Family, own (7 PROVERS)
Dreams, Friends - old (7 PROVERS)
Dreams, Friends - seeing friends (7 PROVERS)
Dreams, Father (5 PROVERS)
Dreams, Funerals (1 PROVER)
Dreams, God, of (1 PROVER)
Dreams, Guidance, advice, looking for (1 PROVER)
Dreams, Grandfather (1 PROVER)
Dreams, Grandmother (1 PROVER)
Dreams, **Half-awake and half-asleep** (4 PROVERS)
Dreams, **Hear her, no one can** (1 PROVER)
Dreams, High Places (3 PROVERS)
Dreams, Historic (3 PROVERS)
Dreams, Homosexuality - open, unabashed (2 PROVERS)
Dreams, House, haunted (1 PROVER)
Dreams, House - youth, like the house of her (3 PROVERS)
Dreams, Invisible, being (1 PROVER)
Dreams, **Light and Dark figures representing good and evil** (1 PROVER)
Dreams, **Looking down from a great height** (2 PROVERS)
Dreams, **Looking for oneself, parent is** (2 PROVERS)
Dreams, Lost, being (1 PROVER)
Dreams, **Midgets, dwarves** (2 PROVERS)
Dreams, Mortification, grief (4 PROVERS)
Dreams, Mother (3 PROVERS)
Dreams, Nakedness (1 PROVER)
Dreams, Parties (3 PROVERS)
Dreams, **Pets** (3 PROVERS)
Dreams, **Play - watching rehearsal** (1 PROVER)
Dreams, Pregnancy (1 PROVER)
Dreams, Rape (1 PROVER)
Dreams, Rape - being raped (1 PROVER)
Dreams, Rape - pursued for rape; being (1 PROVER)
Dreams, Religious (1 PROVER)
Dreams, School (4 PROVERS)
Dreams, School, **teaching** (1 PROVER)
Dreams, School, **being back in** (3 PROVERS)
Dreams, School, **being back in; taking a class about the universe** (1 PROVER)
Dreams, Seduction (3 PROVERS)
Dreams, Seeing again an old schoolmate (4 PROVERS)
Dreams, Sexual (7 PROVERS)

Dreams, Sexual - several people, having sex with (1 PROVER)
Dreams, Sexual - several people, having sex with, indifferent at the same time (1 PROVER)
Dreams, Sexual Identity, ambiguous about one's (2 PROVERS)
Dreams, **Sexual imagery, landscape seen as erotic body** (1 PROVER)
Dreams, **Shadows, of** (1 PROVER)
Dreams, Sister (1 PROVER)
Dreams, **Solar system - its image projected onto the Moon** (1 PROVER)
Dreams, **Spiritual seeking** (3 PROVERS)
Dreams, **Spiritual guide** (4 PROVERS)
Dreams, Teacher, spiritual, of a (1 PROVER)
Dreams, Teaching (1 PROVER)
Dreams, Teaching, **philosophical** (1 PROVER)
Dreams, **Universe, taking a class about** (1 PROVER)
Dreams, **Vertigo** (1 PROVER)
Dreams, **Waking dreams** (1 PROVER)
Dreams, **Young, being again** (1 PROVER)
Dreams, Youth, Time of (3 PROVERS)

VERTIGO

Vertigo, Morning - rising, on (1 PROVER)
Vertigo, Morning - rising, after (1 PROVER)
Vertigo, Accompanied by - **Disorientation** (1 PROVER)
Vertigo, Accompanied by - **Weakness** (1 PROVER)
Vertigo, Continuous (3 PROVERS)
Vertigo, **Earthquake, as if in a** (2 PROVERS)
Vertigo, Exertion, on (1 PROVER)
Vertigo, Falling from a height, as if (1 PROVER)
Vertigo, Floating, as if (2 PROVERS)
Vertigo, Floating, as if - lying, while (1 PROVER)
Vertigo, Floating, as if - **Sides of body** (1 PROVER)
Vertigo, High, places (1 PROVER)
Vertigo, Looking - downward (1 PROVER)
Vertigo, Looking - moving object, at (1 PROVER)
Vertigo, Lying - back, on (1 PROVER)
Vertigo, Lying - down; necessary (1 PROVER)
Vertigo, Lying, amel (1 PROVER)
Vertigo, Nausea - with (1 PROVER)
Vertigo, Objects - approach and then recede, seem to (1 PROVER)
Vertigo, Pregnancy - during (1 PROVER)
Vertigo, Reeling - standing (1 PROVER)
Vertigo, Rising - on (1 PROVER)

Vertigo, Rising - seat, from a (1 PROVER)
Vertigo, Rocking - as if (2 PROVERS)
Vertigo, Rocking - as if, **lying, while** (1 PROVER)
Vertigo, **Rushing sensation - body to head** (1 PROVER)
Vertigo, Sitting - amel. (1 PROVER)
Vertigo, Spin - **head seems to** (1 PROVER)
Vertigo, Standing, on (1 PROVER)
Vertigo, **Tipping, sensation as if ship in storm was tipping in head** (1 PROVER)
Vertigo, Wavelike sensations (3 PROVERS)

HEAD

Head, Congestion - morning, waking, on (5 PROVERS)
Head, Congestion - motion, rapid, from (1 PROVER)
Head, Congestion - Forehead, **right** (1 PROVER)
Head, Constriction (3 PROVERS)
Head, Constriction - air, open agg. (1 PROVER)

Head, Constriction - motion, from (1 PROVER)
Head, Constriction - Forehead (1 PROVER)
Head, **Draining sensation - vertex, from, right ear, to** (1 PROVER)
Head, Fullness (1 PROVER)
Head, Fullness - rising on (1 PROVER)
Head, Fullness - **walking agg.** (1 PROVER)
Head, Heaviness (4 PROVERS)
Head, Heaviness - **left** (1 PROVER)
Head, Heaviness - morning, waking, on (2 PROVERS)
Head, Itching (4 PROVERS)
Head, Itching - crawling (1 PROVER)
Head, Itching - Sides, right (2 PROVERS)
Head, Itching - Sides, left (1 PROVER)
Head, Itching - Vertex (1 PROVER)
Head, Lump - sensation as from a - **Vertex, in** (1 PROVER)
Head, **Metal sheet - sensation of, Forehead, in** (1 PROVER)
Head, Opening - **Frontal sinuses** (2 PROVERS)
Head, Opening - **Frontal sinuses, morning, waking, on** (1 PROVER)
Head, Opening - **sensation as if opening, left side** (1 PROVER)
Head, Opening - **sensation as if opening, capillaries, in** (1 PROVER)
Head, Opening - **sensation as if opening, vertex, at** (1 PROVER)
Head, Pain - (12 PROVERS)
Head, Pain - morning, waking on (5 PROVERS)
Head, Pain - light, general, from light in (1 PROVER)
Head, Pain - Odors, strong, from (2 PROVERS)
Head, Pain - Pressure, external amel. (3 PROVERS)

Head, Pain - Running, from (1 PROVER)
Head, Pain - Tobacco, from (2 PROVERS)
Head, Pain - Eyes, **extending to jaw** (1 PROVER)
Head, Pain - Eyes, **behind, left** (1 PROVER)
Head, Pain - Eyes, **behind, right** (1 PROVER)
Head, Pain - Forehead (5 PROVERS)
Head, Pain - Forehead, right (4 PROVERS)
Head, Pain - Forehead, extending to Temples (3 PROVERS)
Head, Pain - Nose, above root of (1 PROVER)
Head, Pain - Occiput (2 PROVERS)
Head, Pain - Occiput, extending to, Neck (1 PROVER)
Head, Pain - Sides (4 PROVERS)
Head, Pain - Sides, left (3 PROVERS)
Head, Pain - Temples (6 PROVERS)
Head, Pain - Temples, left (2 PROVERS)
Head, Pain - Temples and Forehead (5 PROVERS)
Head, Pain - Vertex (3 PROVERS)
Head, Pain - boring (1 PROVER)
Head, Pain - burning, Vertex (1 PROVER)
Head, Pain - cutting (2 PROVERS)
Head, Pain - cutting, Forehead (1 PROVER)
Head, Pain - dull, Forehead (2 PROVERS)
Head, Pain - dull, Forehead, right (2 PROVERS)
Head, Pain - dull, Sides (1 PROVER)
Head, Pain - dull, Temples (2 PROVERS)
Head, Pain - dull, Temples, right (1 PROVER)
Head, Pain - dull, **Temples and Forehead** (4 PROVERS)
Head, Pain - pressing (6 PROVERS)
Head, Pain - pressing, light agg. (1 PROVER)
Head, Pain - pressing, Eyes, behind, left (1 PROVER)
Head, Pain - pressing, Eyes, behind, right (1 PROVER)
Head, Pain - pressing, Forehead, Eminence, frontal (2 PROVERS)
Head, Pain - pressing, Forehead - Eyes - Over, right (1 PROVER)
Head, Pain - pressing, Temples (3 PROVERS)
Head, Pain - pressing, Temples, **right then left** (1 PROVER)
Head, Pain - pressing, Vertex (1 PROVER)
Head, Pain - pulsating (4 PROVERS)
Head, Pain - pulsating, Forehead extending to Temples (2 PROVERS)
Head, Pain - pulsating **with beat of heart** (1 PROVER)
Head, Pulsating (5 PROVERS)
Head, Tingling - **wavelike, through head** (1 PROVER)
Head, **Vibration - wavelike, through head** (1 PROVER)
Head, Waving sensation (1 PROVER)

EYE

Eye, Closing the eyes - desire to (2 PROVERS)
Eye, Closing the eyes - must close, sunlight, from (1 PROVER)
Eye, Closing the eyes - **partial closing** (1 PROVER)
Eye, Discoloration - red (3 PROVERS)
Eye, Discoloration - red, Lids, right (2 PROVERS)
Eye, Dryness (4 PROVERS)
Eye, Dryness - left (1 PROVER)
Eye, Dryness - morning, waking, on (1 PROVER)
Eye, Heaviness (2 PROVERS)
Eye, Injected (2 PROVERS)
Eye, Itching (5 PROVERS)
Eye, Itching - left (3 PROVERS)
Eye, Itching - right (2 PROVERS)
Eye, Itching - Canthi, Inner, left (2 PROVERS)
Eye, Itching - Lids, **right** (1 PROVER)
Eye, Irritation - **Canthi** (1 PROVER)
Eye, Lachrymation (4 PROVERS)
Eye, Lachrymation - right (1 PROVER)
Eye, Lachrymation - left (2 PROVERS)
Eye, Open eyelids - sensation as if wide open (1 PROVER)
Eye, Opening the eyelids - closing in quick succession, and (1 PROVER)
Eye, Opening the eyelids - difficult (1 PROVER)
Eye, Pain (6 PROVERS)
Eye, Pain - Canthi (2 PROVERS)
Eye, Pain - Canthi, outer, **extending to vertex** (1 PROVER)
Eye, Pain - burning (5 PROVERS)
Eye, Pain - burning, left (2 PROVERS)
Eye, Pain - burning, Canthi, in (1 PROVER)
Eye, Pain - drawing, extending to vertex (1 PROVER)
Eye, Pain - pressing, outward (1 PROVER)
Eye, Pain - stinging (1 PROVER)
Eye, Pain - stitching, left (1 PROVER)
Eye, Photophobia (4 PROVERS)
Eye, Photophobia - sunlight (1 PROVER)
Eye, Protrusion - sensation of (1 PROVER)
Eye, Strain (1 PROVER)
Eye, Tension (1 PROVER)
Eye, Swelling - right (2 PROVERS)
Eye, Swelling - sensation of (1 PROVER)
Eye, Tired sensation (4 PROVERS)
Eye, Tired sensation - closing the eyes amel. (1 PROVER)

VISION

Vision, Acute (2 PROVERS)
Vision, Approach and then recede - objects seem to (1 PROVER)
Vision, Blurred (3 PROVERS)
Vision, Illusions of - Motion, of (1 PROVER)
Vision, Illusions of - Light, yellow and green (1 PROVER)
Vision, Loss of vision - **sensation of** (2 PROVERS)
Vision, Loss of vision - **sensation of, peripheral** (1 PROVER)
Vision, Loss of vision - **sensation of, left side** (1 PROVER)
Vision, Weak (2 PROVERS)

EAR

Ear, Discoloration - redness, left (1 PROVER)
Ear, Fullness, sensation of (5 PROVERS)
Ear, Fullness, sensation of - **left** (2 PROVERS)
Ear, Heat- left (1 PROVER)
Ear, Heat - **sensation of, Ear, inside, left** (1 PROVER)
Ear, Itching - Concha (1 PROVER)
Ear, Noises (2 PROVERS)
Ear, Noises - crackling (1 PROVER)
Ear, Opening, sensation of (1 PROVER)
Ear, Pain (6 PROVERS)
Ear, Pain - morning, waking on (1 PROVER)
Ear, Pain - Concha (3 PROVERS)
Ear, Pain - touch, on (3 PROVERS)
Ear, Pain - **wavelike** (1 PROVER)
Ear, Pain - Behind the ear (1 PROVER)
Ear, Pain - burning (2 PROVERS)
Ear, Pain - pressing (4 PROVERS)
Ear, Pain - pressing, extending to **jaw** (2 PROVERS)
Ear, Pulsation - Eardrum, sensation in (1 PROVER)

HEARING

Hearing, Acute (2 PROVERS)
Hearing, Acute - noises to, high-pitched (1 PROVER)

NOSE

Nose, **Air - flowing through bridge of nose, sensation of** (1 PROVER)
Nose, Congestion (4 PROVERS)
Nose, Congestion - **left** (3 PROVERS)

Nose, Congestion - **bathing, hot amel.** (1 PROVER)
Nose, Congestion - **hot drinks amel.** (1 PROVER)
Nose, Congestion - morning, waking (1 PROVER)
Nose, Coryza (6 PROVERS)
Nose, Coryza - morning, waking (1 PROVER)
Nose, Coryza - discharge, with (4 PROVERS)
Nose, Coryza - discharge, without (2 PROVERS)
Nose, Discharge (6 PROVERS)
Nose, Discharge - one side (2 PROVERS)
Nose, Discharge - left (2 PROVERS)
Nose, Discharge - morning, **waking, on** (2 PROVERS)
Nose, Discharge - bloody (2 PROVERS)
Nose, Discharge - clear (5 PROVERS)
Nose, Discharge - watery (7 PROVERS)
Nose, Discharge - yellow (2 PROVERS)
Nose, Itching (4 PROVERS)
Nose, Itching - Nostrils, Inside (2 PROVERS)
Nose, Long - sensation as if elongated (1 PROVER)
Nose, Obstruction (5 PROVERS)
Nose, Obstruction - one side (4 PROVERS)
Nose, Obstruction - left (4 PROVERS)
Nose, Obstruction - morning, waking, on (1 PROVER)
Nose, Obstruction - lying, side on which he is lying (1 PROVER)
Nose, Obstruction - sensation of (1 PROVER)
Nose, Odors (4 PROVERS)
Nose, Odors - **flowers, of** (1 PROVER)
Nose, Odors - food, of (1 PROVER)
Nose, Odors - **mothballs, of** (1 PROVER)
Nose, Odors - putrid, of (1 PROVER)
Nose, Odors - smoke, of (1 PROVER)
Nose, Obstruction - one side (1 PROVER)
Nose, Obstruction - one side, **left** (1 PROVER)
Nose, Open - sensation as if (3 PROVERS)
Nose, Open - sensation as if, **left** (1 PROVER)
Nose, Pain - Nostrils, left (1 PROVER)
Nose, Pain - burning (2 PROVERS)
Nose, Pain - burning, **morning, waking, on** (1 PROVER)
Nose, Pain - burning, Nostrils, inside (1 PROVER)
Nose, Pain - drawing, extending to **occiput** (1 PROVER)
Nose, Smell - acute (3 PROVERS)
Nose, Smell - acute, everything smells too strong (3 PROVERS)
Nose, Sneezing (4 PROVERS)
Nose, Sneezing - **drinking, from** (1 PROVER)
Nose, Swelling - Inside, **sensation of** (1 PROVER)

FACE

Face, Air - **flowing through face, sensation of** (1 PROVER)
Face, Clenched jaw (1 PROVER)
Face, Clenching jaw, grinding of teeth; with (1 PROVER)
Face, Cracking - **Sinuses, Maxillary in** (1 PROVER)
Face, **Crunching noise - Jaws, when closing jaws** (1 PROVER)
Face, Discoloration - red (2 PROVERS)
Face, Discoloration - red, Cheeks (2 PROVERS)
Face, Discoloration - red, Cheeks, blotches (1 PROVER)
Face, Dryness - lips (2 PROVERS)
Face, Eruptions - (6 PROVERS)
Face, Eruptions - painful, Nose (1 PROVER)
Face, Eruptions - Cheek (4 PROVERS)
Face, Eruptions - Chin (2 PROVERS)
Face, Eruptions - Forehead (3 PROVERS)
Face, Eruptions - Lips, upper (2 PROVERS)
Face, Eruptions - Nose (2 PROVERS)
Face, Eruptions - Nose, septum (1 PROVER)
Face, Eruptions - pimples (3 PROVERS)
Face, Eruptions - pimples, painful to touch (1 PROVER)
Face, Eruptions - pimples, **tingling** (1 PROVER)
Face, Eruptions - pimples, Cheek (2 PROVERS)
Face, Eruptions - pimples, Chin (1 PROVER)
Face, Eruptions - pimples, Lips, upper (2 PROVERS)
Face, Eruptions - pimples, Forehead (2 PROVERS)
Face, Eruptions - pimples, Forehead, **eyebrows** (2 PROVERS)
Face, Eruptions -rash (2 PROVERS)
Face, Eruptions - rash, Forehead (1 PROVER)
Face, Eruptions - rash, Cheek (2 PROVERS)
Face, Eruptions - rash, Chin (1 PROVER)
Face, Eruptions - red (1 PROVER)
Face, Eruptions - red, Lips, **upper** (3 PROVERS)
Face, **Expansion, opening up - Sinuses, in** (1 PROVER)
Face, Fullness - **Lip, lower, sensation of** (1 PROVER)
Face, Heat - sensation of, (2 PROVERS)
Face, Inflammation - Sinuses (2 PROVERS)
Face, Itching - Mouth, Corners, of (2 PROVERS)
Face, Pain (1 PROVER)
Face, Pain - numbness with (1 PROVER)
Face, Pain - Eye, below [= infraorbital] (1 PROVER)
Face, Pain - Jaw, Articulation (2 PROVERS)
Face, Pain - Jaw, Articulation, left (1 PROVER)
Face, Pain - Jaw, Articulation, morning (1 PROVER)
Face, Pain - Jaw, Lower Jaw (2 PROVERS)

Face, Pain - Jaw, Lower Jaw, **extending to teeth** (1 PROVER)
Face, Pain - Jaw, Lower Jaw, **radiating** (1 PROVER)
Face, Pain - Sinuses, Frontal (6 PROVERS)
Face, Pain - Sinuses Frontal, **left** (3 PROVERS)
Face, Pain - Sinuses, Frontal, **left to right** (1 PROVER)
Face Pain - Sinuses, Maxillary (2 PROVERS)
Face, Pain - Sinuses, Maxillary, **extending to teeth** (1 PROVER)
Face, Pain - cutting, Sinuses, Frontal (1 PROVER)
Face, Pain, pressing (1 PROVER)
Face, Pain - pressing, Jaws, Articulation of jaw (2 PROVERS)
Face, Pain - pressing, Jaws, Lower (1 PROVER)
Face, Pain - pressing, Jaws, Lower, extending to Chin (1 PROVER)
Face, Pain - pressing, Jaws, Lower, extending to Angle of jaw (1 PROVER)
Face, Pain - pressing, Jaws, Lower, extending to Ear (1 PROVER)
Face, Pain - pressing, Jaws, Lower, extending to **Malar bones** (1 PROVER)
Face, Pain - pressing, Malar bones (2 PROVERS)
Face, Pain - pressing, Sinuses, Frontal, **left** (1 PROVER)
Face, Pain - pressing, Sinuses, Maxillary (2 PROVERS)
Face, Pain, pressing, Chin, under chin (1 PROVER)
Face, Pain - stinging, **Cheek, left** (1 PROVER)
Face, Pain - stitching (2 PROVERS)
Face, Pain - stitching, extending to: Temple (1 PROVER)
Face, Pain - stitching, left (1 PROVER)
Face, Pain, stitching, Upper (1 PROVER)
Face, Pain, stitching, Upper, **Upper lip, extending to temple** (1 PROVER)
Face, Stiffness - Jaws, Lower (1 PROVER)
Face, Tingling (1 PROVER)
Face, Tingling - lips (3 PROVERS)
Face, Tingling - lips, upper (2 PROVERS)
Face, Tingling - lips, upper, **extending backward into head** (1 PROVER)
Face, Tingling - lips, upper, **left** (1 PROVER)
Face, Tingling - lips, lower (1 PROVER)
Face, **Vibration - lip, upper, extending backward into head** (1 PROVER)
Face, **Vibration, wavelike** (1 PROVER)
Face, Tic (1 PROVER)

MOUTH

Mouth, Dryness (3 PROVERS)
Mouth, Dryness - thirst, with (2 PROVERS)
Mouth, Dryness - lips (2 PROVERS)
Mouth, Enlarged - Tongue, sensation as if (1 PROVER)

Mouth, Eruptions - vesicles, Gums (1 PROVER)
Mouth, Numbness - Tongue (1 PROVER)
Mouth, Salivation (1 PROVER)
Mouth, Salivation - **electric sensation, with** (1 PROVER)
Mouth, Swelling - Tongue, sensation of (1 PROVER)
Mouth, Taste - wanting (2 PROVERS)
Mouth, **Tingling** (6 PROVERS)
Mouth, **Tingling - morning, waking on** (1 PROVER)
Mouth, **Tingling - extending to, ear** (1 PROVER)
Mouth, **Tingling - inner lining** (1 PROVER)
Mouth, **Tingling - tongue** (2 PROVERS)
Mouth, **Tingling - lips** (3 PROVERS)
Mouth, **Tingling - lips, upper, left** (2 PROVERS)
Mouth, **Tingling - lips, lower** (1 PROVER)
Mouth, Ulcers - canker sore (3 PROVERS)
Mouth, **Vibration** (1 PROVER)

THROAT

Throat, Constriction (2 PROVERS)
Throat, Constriction - swallowing difficult (1 PROVER)
Throat, **Draining - sensation of sinuses draining through throat** (1 PROVER)
Throat, Dryness (3 PROVERS)
Throat, Hawk, disposition to - talking, before being able to (1 PROVER)
Throat, Heat (1 PROVER)
Throat, Itching (1 PROVER)
Throat, Pain (8 PROVERS)
Throat, Pain - left (1 PROVER)
Throat, Pain - left, extending to Ears (1 PROVER)
Throat, Pain - extending to Ear (1 PROVER)
Throat, Pain - extending downward (1 PROVER)
Throat, Pain - burning (1 PROVER)
Throat, Pain - sore (4 PROVERS)
Throat, Pain - sore, left (2 PROVERS)
Throat, Pain - sore, swallowing, on (1 PROVER)
Throat, Pain - sore, morning, waking, on (3 PROVERS)
Throat, Scraping (4 PROVERS)
Throat, Scraping - **cold drinks amel.** (1 PROVER)
Throat, Swallowing - difficult (1 PROVER)
Throat, Swelling - sensation of (2 PROVERS)
Throat, Tickling (3 PROVERS)
Throat, Tickling - cough **amel.** (1 PROVER)

STOMACH

Stomach, Acidity (1 PROVER)
Stomach, Appetite - wanting (5 PROVERS)
Stomach, **Churning sensation** (1 PROVER)
Stomach, Bubbling - **sensation of food rising, with** (1 PROVER)
Stomach, Distention (4 PROVERS)
Stomach, Distension - eating, after (2 PROVERS)
Stomach, Distension - painful (1 PROVER)
Stomach, Emptiness, **as if** (1 PROVER)
Stomach, Eructations (6 PROVERS)
Stomach, Eructations - **bending forward agg.** (1 PROVER)
Stomach, Flatulence, **sensation of** (4 PROVERS)
Stomach, Gagging - Coughing, from (1 PROVER)
Stomach, **Hollow, sensation as if** (1 PROVER)
Stomach, Indigestion (2 PROVERS)
Stomach, Nausea (7 PROVERS)
Stomach, Nausea - morning (2 PROVERS)
Stomach, Nausea - morning, waking on (2 PROVERS)
Stomach, Nausea - drinking amel. (1 PROVER)
Stomach, Nausea - eating, while (1 PROVER)
Stomach, Nausea - eating amel. (2 PROVERS)
Stomach, Nausea - tobacco, smoking (1 PROVER)
Stomach, Nausea - urination amel. (1 PROVER)
Stomach, Nausea - **extending upward** (1 PROVER)
Stomach, Nausea - **extending to, Ears** (1 PROVER)
Stomach, Nausea - **extending to, Salivary glands** (1 PROVER)
Stomach, Pain - cramping (1 PROVER)
Stomach, Pain, burning (1 PROVER)
Stomach, Rumbling (2 PROVERS)
Stomach, sinking, sensation of (1 PROVER)
Stomach, Retraction - sensation of (2 PROVERS)
Stomach, Thirsty (3 PROVERS)
Stomach, **Wavelike sensation** (1 PROVER)

ABDOMEN

Abdomen, Coldness (1 PROVER)
Abdomen, Distension (3 PROVERS)
Abdomen, Flatulence (4 PROVERS)
Abdomen, Flatulence - morning, waking on (1 PROVER)
Abdomen, Flatulence - afternoon (1 PROVER)
Abdomen, Flatulence - eating, after (2 PROVERS)
Abdomen, Flatulence - **emotions, from** (1 PROVER)

Abdomen, Flatulence - eructations amel. (1 PROVER)
Abdomen, Flatulence, painful (2 PROVERS)
Abdomen, Fullness, sensation of (1 PROVER)
Abdomen, Itching (1 PROVER)
Abdomen, Pain, eructations amel. (2 PROVERS)
Abdomen, Pain, flatus amel. (1 PROVER)
Abdomen, Pain - cramping (4 PROVERS)
Abdomen, Pain - cramping, sudden (1 PROVER)
Abdomen, Pain - cramping, Morning, waking, on (1 PROVER)
Abdomen, Pain - cramping, Umbilicus, region of (1 PROVER)
Abdomen, Pain - cutting (2 PROVERS)
Abdomen, Pain - cutting, Umbilicus, region of (1 PROVER)
Abdomen, Rumbling - **Umbilicus, around** (1 PROVER)
Abdomen, Retraction - sensation of (2 PROVERS)
Abdomen, Sinking, sensation of (1 PROVER)
Abdomen, Swelling - Abdomen, of (3 PROVERS)
Abdomen, Swelling - Abdomen, of, **morning, waking, on** (1 PROVER)

RECTUM

Rectum, Constipation (3 PROVERS)
Rectum, Constipation - ineffectual urging and straining (2 PROVERS)
Rectum, Flatus (1 PROVER)
Rectum, Inactivity of rectum (2 PROVERS)

STOOL

Stool, Dark (3 PROVERS)
Stool, Forcible (2 PROVERS)
Stool, Hard (2 PROVERS)
Stool, Soft (2 PROVERS)

FEMALE GENITALIA

Female genitalia, Itching - Vagina (2 PROVERS)
Female genitalia, Menses - bright red (1 PROVER)
Female genitalia, Menses - copious (1 PROVER)
Female genitalia, Menses - copious, night (1 PROVER)
Female genitalia, Menses - scanty (2 PROVERS)
Female genitalia, Menses - return, ceased, **after the regular period has** (1 PROVER)
Female genitalia, Menses - return, ceased, after the regular menstrual cycle has (1 PROVER)
Female genitalia, Menses - thin (1 PROVER)
Female genitalia, Sexual desire - increased (1 PROVER)

LARYNX AND TRACHEA

Larynx, Cold sensation - on breathing (1 PROVER)

RESPIRATION

Respiration, Catching - cough, **amel.** (1 PROVER)
Respiration, Catching - cough, from (1 PROVER)

COUGH

Cough, Asthmatic (2 PROVERS)
Cough, Cold - air (1 PROVER)
Cough, Cold - air, sensation of icy cold air in air passages, from (1 PROVER)
Cough, Constriction - Chest, in (1 PROVER)
Cough, **Cramping** (1 PROVER)
Cough, Drinks - cold (2 PROVERS)
Cough, Dry (3 PROVERS)

Cough, Eating - from (1 PROVER)
Cough, Eating - from, **gagging, with** (1 PROVER)
Cough, Mucus - Larynx (1 PROVER)
Cough, Sitting (1 PROVER)
Cough, Irritable (2 PROVERS)
Cough, Irritation - Larynx, in (1 PROVER)
Cough, Painful (2 PROVERS)
Cough, Paroxysmal (2 PROVERS)
Cough, Paroxysmal - attacks follow one another quickly (1 PROVER)
Cough, Racking (2 PROVERS)
Cough, Sudden (1 PROVER)
Cough, Tickling (3 PROVERS)
Cough, Tickling - Chest, Upper in (1 PROVER)
Cough, Tickling - Larynx (2 PROVERS)
Cough, Violent (2 PROVERS)
Cough, Violent - **blowing nose, from** (1 PROVER)
Cough, Violent - **drinking, from** (1 PROVER)
Cough, Violent - jerking **of body, with** (2 PROVERS)

EXPECTORATION

Expectoration, Difficult (2 PROVERS)

CHEST

Chest, Anxiety (3 PROVERS)
Chest, Anxiety - Region of Heart (1 PROVER)
Chest, Anxiety - Region of heart, thinking of it agg. (1 PROVER)

Chest, Pain (7 PROVERS)
Chest, Pain - Axilla (2 PROVERS)
Chest, Pain - Axilla, **left** (2 PROVERS)
Chest, Pain - Mammae, paroxysmal (3 PROVERS)
Chest, Pain - Mammae (4 PROVERS)
Chest, Pain - Mammae, right (2 PROVERS)
Chest, Pain - Mammae, left (1 PROVER)
Chest, Pain - Mammae, extending to **Heart** (1 PROVER)
Chest, Pain - Mammae, Nipples, **above** (1 PROVER)
Chest, Pain - aching, Mammae (1 PROVER)
Chest, Pain - burning (4 PROVERS)
Chest, Pain - burning, Mammae, Nipples, **above** (1 PROVER)
Chest, Pain - burning, Axilla (2 PROVERS)
Chest, Pain - burning, Axilla, **left** (2 PROVERS)
Chest, Pain - burning, Heart (1 PROVER)
Chest, Pain - stitching (3 PROVERS)
Chest, Pain - stitching, Mammae (3 PROVERS)
Chest, Pain - stitching, Mammae, left (1 PROVER)
Chest, Pain - stitching, Mammae, under (1 PROVER)
Chest, Pain - stitching, Mammae, Nipple (1 PROVER)
Chest, Pain - stitching, Mammae, Nipple, right (1 PROVER)
Chest, Pain - stitching, sides, left, extending to heart (1 PROVER)
Chest, Palpitation of Heart (2 PROVERS)
Chest, Constriction, Chest, in (4 PROVERS)
Chest, Constriction - band, as if (1 PROVER)
Chest, Constriction - Sternum (1 PROVER)
Chest, Constriction - Sternum, **eructation amel.** (1 PROVER)
Chest, Clothing agg. (1 PROVER)
Chest, **Expansion - Lungs, sensation as if** (2 PROVERS)
Chest, Tickling in - Sternum, **around** (1 PROVER)
Chest, Tingling in - Lungs (1 PROVER)
Chest, Warmth, sensation of - **Sides** (1 PROVER)
Chest, Warmth, sensation of - **Axilla** (1 PROVER)

BACK

Back, Bubbling sensation in - **Spine** (1 PROVER)
Back, Buzzing sensation - **Lumbar region** (1 PROVER)
Back, Elongated, **neck, as if** (1 PROVER)
Back, Pain (6 PROVERS)
Back, Pain - Cervical region (2 PROVERS)
Back, Pain - Cervical region, extending to: Shoulders (1 PROVER)
Back, Pain - Cervical region, extending to: down the back (1 PROVER)
Back, Pain - Dorsal region (3 PROVERS)

Back, Pain - Dorsal region, Scapulae, between (2 PROVERS)
Back, Pain - Dorsal region, Scapulae, right - Under (1 PROVER)
Back, Pain - Dorsal region, Scapulae, Between (1 PROVER)
Back, Pain - Lumbar region, right (1 PROVER)
Back, Pain - Lumbar region, sitting, while (1 PROVER)
Back, Pain - aching (4 PROVERS)
Back, Pain - aching, Cervical region (2 PROVERS)
Back, Pain - aching, Dorsal region, Scapulae, right, under (1 PROVER)
Back, Pain - aching, Dorsal region Scapulae, Between (1 PROVER)
Back, Pain - aching, Lumbar region, right (1 PROVER)
Back, Pain - burning, Spine (1 PROVER)
Back, Pain - burning, Dorsal region, Scapulae, Between (1 PROVER)
Back, Pain - dull, Cervical region (1 PROVER)
Back, Pain - dull, Cervical region, **shoulder, near** (1 PROVER)
Back, Pain - pressing, Dorsal Region, Scapulae, between (1 PROVER)
Back, Pain - sore, Cervical region, extending to: **Fourth dorsal vertebra** (1 PROVER)
Back, Pain - sore, Cervical region, **extending to Shoulders** (1 PROVER)

Back, Pain - stitching, Dorsal region, motion on (1 PROVER)
Back, Pain - stitching, Dorsal region, Scapulae, right, under (1 PROVER)
Back, Pain - stitching, Dorsal Region, Scapulae between, moving (1 PROVER)
Back, Pain - stitching, Dorsal Region, Scapulae, standing, while (1 PROVER)
Back, Pain - stitching, Dorsal Region, Scapulae, **shoulders pulled back** (1 PROVER)
Back, Tension, Scapulae (1 PROVER)
Back, Spasms, Lumbar region (1 PROVER)
Back. Stiffness - Cervical region (3 PROVERS)
Back, Stiffness - Cervical region, morning, rising, after (1 PROVER)
Back, Stiffness - Cervical region, extending **downward along spine** (1 PROVER)
Back, Stiffness - Dorsal region, extending **downward along spine** (1 PROVER)
Back, **Vibration, Lumbar region, small spot** (1 PROVER)

EXTREMITIES

Extremities, Coldness - Foot, icy cold (1 PROVER)
Extremities, Coldness - Thigh (1 PROVER)
Extremities, Convulsion - one side (1 PROVER)
Extremities, **Convulsion - one side, side not lain on** (1 PROVER)
Extremities, Convulsion - Shoulder, small spot (1 PROVER)
Extremities, Dryness - Hands (2 PROVERS)
Extremities, **Eruptions - red, spots** (2 PROVERS)
Extremities, Eruptions - itching (4 PROVERS)
Extremities, Eruptions - Elbow, elevations (1 PROVER)
Extremities, Eruptions - Elbow, itching (1 PROVER)
Extremities, Eruptions - Hand, Back of, elevations (1 PROVER)
Extremities, Eruptions - Hand, Back of, itching (1 PROVER)

Extremities, Heaviness - Lower limbs, walking, while (2 PROVERS)
Extremities, **Itching (hands and feet)** (4 PROVERS)
Extremities, Itching - Hand (1 PROVER)
Extremities, Itching - Palm (2 PROVERS)
Extremities, Itching - Wrist, Inner side (1 PROVER)
Extremities, Itching - Fingers, First finger, Joints, Distal (1 PROVER)
Extremities, Itching - Ankle (right) (1 PROVER)
Extremities, **Jerking - lying, while, one side, side not lain on** (1 PROVER)
Extremities, Pain - Shoulder, sudden (1 PROVER)
Extremities, Pain - Shoulder, dislocation, as from (1 PROVER)
Extremities, Pain - Shoulder, extending to Forearm (1 PROVER)
Extremities, Pain - Shoulder, motion, sudden agg. (1 PROVER)
Extremities, Pain - Shoulder, continued motion amel. (1 PROVER)
Extremities, Pain - sore, Shoulder, extending to Forearm (1 PROVER)
Extremities, Pain - sore, Shoulder, extending to Neck (1 PROVER)
Extremities, Pain -sore, Thigh (1 PROVER)
Extremities, Pain -sore, Thigh, walking, while (1 PROVER)
Extremities, Pain - sore, Ankle (2 PROVERS)
Extremities, Pain - Ankle (3 PROVERS)
Extremities, Pain - sprained, as if, Ankle (2 PROVERS)
Extremities, Pain - sprained, as if, Ankle, extending to foot (1 PROVER)
Extremities, Pain - sprained, Toe (1 PROVER)
Extremities, Pain - Toe (3 PROVERS)
Extremities, Pain - Foot, standing, while (1 PROVER)
Extremities, Pain - stitching, Toes (1 PROVER)
Extremities, Pain - burning, Shoulder (left) (1 PROVER)
Extremities, Pain - burning, Elbow, Bend of (1 PROVER)
Extremities, Pain - burning, Hand, Palm (2 PROVERS)
Extremities, Pain - stinging, Hand, Palm (right) (1 PROVER)
Extremities, Pain - drawing, Upper arm, extending to downward (1 PROVER)
Extremities, Pain - pressing, Knee (1 PROVER)
Extremities, Pulsation - Shoulder (1 PROVER)
Extremities, Pulsation - Wrist (1 PROVER)
Extremities, Stiffness - Lower limbs (1 PROVER)
Extremities, Tingling (6 PROVERS)
Extremities, Tingling - Fingers (1 PROVER)
Extremities, Tingling - Hand (3 PROVERS)
Extremities, Tingling - Lower limbs (2 PROVERS)
Extremities, Tingling - Lower limbs, extending to, downward (1 PROVER)
Extremities, Trembling (2 PROVERS)
Extremities, Trembling - Shoulder (1 PROVER)
Extremities, Trembling - Thigh, extending upward and downward (1 PROVER)
Extremities, Weakness - Upper limbs (2 PROVERS)
Extremities, Weakness -Hand (1 PROVER)

Extremities, Weakness - Lower limbs (2 PROVERS)
Extremities, Weakness - Knee (1 PROVER)

SLEEP

Sleep, Dreaming - **half-awake, while** (2 PROVERS)
Sleep, Semi-conscious (2 PROVERS)
Sleep, Sleeplessness - protracted (1 PROVER)
Sleep, Sleeplessness - waking, after (3 PROVERS)
Sleep, Sleepiness - sudden (3 PROVERS)
Sleep, Sleepiness - daytime (6 PROVERS)
Sleep, Unrefreshing - rising, indisposed to (5 PROVERS)
Sleep, Waking - dreams, from (4 PROVERS)
Sleep, Waking - paralyzed feeling, with (1 PROVER)
Sleep, **Waking - sudden, as if startled** (3 PROVERS)
Sleep, Waking - as from fright (2 PROVERS)
Sleep, Waking - too early (4 PROVERS)

Sleep, Waking - night - midnight - after, 1 h (1 PROVER)
Sleep, Waking - night - midnight - after, 2:30 h (2 PROVERS)
Sleep, Waking - night - midnight - after, 3 h (2 PROVERS)
Sleep, Waking - night - midnight - after, 3:30 h (1 PROVER)

CHILL

Chill, Morning (1 PROVER)
Chill, Forenoon - 11 h (1 PROVER)
Chill, Chilliness - upper body (2 PROVERS)
Chill, Chilliness (4 PROVERS)
Chill, Internal, (3 PROVERS)
Chill, Internal, coldness, bones in (1 PROVER)
Chill, External (3 PROVERS)
Chill, Icy coldness of body (2 PROVERS)
Chill, Shaking (1 PROVER)
Chill, **Beginning - feet, in, moving upward through body** (2 PROVERS)

FEVER

Fever, Alternating with - chills (1 PROVER)

SKIN

Skin, **Air - flowing in and out through, sensation as if** (1 PROVER)
Skin, Coldness - upper part of body (2 PROVERS)
Skin, Coldness (1 PROVER)
Skin, Eruptions - itching (1 PROVER)

Skin, Eruptions - red (3 PROVERS)
Skin, Eruptions, pimples (1 PROVER)
Skin, Itching (5 PROVERS)
Skin, Pain, Stinging (1 PROVER)

GENERALS

Generals, Morning, waking on (8 PROVERS)
Generals, Air, open amel (1 PROVER)
Generals, Anxiety, general physical (1 PROVER)
Generals, Anxiety, general physical, acc. by Heat, sensation of (1 PROVER)
Generals, **Cold - feeling, upper body** (2 PROVERS)
Generals, Cold - feeling (1 PROVER)
Generals, Cold - feeling, bones in (1 PROVER)
Generals, Collapse (1 PROVER)
Generals, Emaciation (5 PROVERS)
Generals, Energy - excess of energy (4 PROVERS)
Generals, Energy - excess of energy, smoking amel. (1 PROVER) 193
Generals, Faintness - accompanied by, nausea (1 PROVER)
Generals, Food and drinks - ice cream, desire (2 PROVERS)
Generals, Food and drinks - salt, desire (2 PROVERS)
Generals, Food and drinks - sweets, desire (2 PROVERS)
Generals, Heat - sensation of (1 PROVER)
Generals, Itching (7 PROVERS)
Generals, Pain - appear suddenly (1 PROVER)
Generals, Pain - appear suddenly, disappear suddenly, and (1 PROVER)
Generals, Pain - burning (10 PROVERS)
Generals, Pain - stinging, Externally (6 PROVERS)
Generals, Pain - stinging, Externally, left side (1 PROVER)
Generals, Pain - stitching (6 PROVERS)
Generals, Paralysis - sensation of (2 PROVERS)
Generals, **Paralysis - sensation of, on waking** (1 PROVER)
Generals, Pulsation - Internally (4 PROVERS)
Generals, Pulsation - **Internally, blood vessels, acc. by wavelike sensations** (2 PROVERS)
Generals, Pulsation - **Internally, blood vessels, shakes body** (2 PROVERS)
Generals, Pulse - sensation of, **reverberation throughout body** (3 PROVERS)
Generals, Pulse - sensation of, **reverberating throughout body,** closing eyes agg. (1 PROVER)
Generals, Relaxation - physical (3 PROVERS)
Generals, Relaxation - Muscles, of (1 PROVER)
Generals, Restlessness (4 PROVERS)
Generals, Side - one side (10 PROVERS)
Generals, Side - left (8 PROVERS)

Generals, Sudden manifestation (6 PROVERS)
Generals, Sun - **desires** (1 PROVER)
Generals, Tingling (10 PROVERS)
Generals, **Tingling, flowing over body, sensation of** (1 PROVER)
Generals, Tingling, left side (1 PROVER)
Generals, Trembling, Externally (1 PROVER)
Generals, Vibration (5 PROVERS)
Generals, Wavelike sensations (6 PROVER)
Generals, Weakness (5 PROVERS)
Generals, Weakness, vertigo with (1 PROVER)
Generals, Weakness - walking (1 PROVER)
Generals, Weakness - nausea, with (2 PROVERS)
Generals, Weakness - sudden (1 PROVER)
Generals, Weariness (10 PROVERS)
Generals, Weariness - sudden (2 PROVERS)
Generals, Weariness -morning, on waking (5 PROVERS)
Generals, Weariness - walking (2 PROVERS)
Generals, Weather - foggy weather amel (1 PROVER; NEW RUBRIC)
Generals, Weather - cold, wet amel (1 PROVERS)

Chapter Eight

A Tabacum Case

Male 63 years old.

He came complaining of a chronic back problem. He had surgery in 1991 and is considering having another operation.

Two year ago I was fine, I was going to the gym and running. Beginning last year it got worse. Last summer was really bad and now it's really bad. I feel out of shape, twisted, a fusion has been suggested.

Meanwhile I have to deal with my mental state. I'm an artist, self-employed, making a living. Two to three years ago very suddenly my sleep was changing. It was a strange feeling. I started to drool. I feel like I am drooling.

It's the opposite to 3 years ago where I had a totally dry mouth. I get bad sleep.

I try to sleep 12-1 a.m. I try to get 6 hours but it's always a problem in my life.

I don't smoke, drink is normal.

At age 10 I went into a comatose state from nephritis of the kidney. Now I'm fine. At 17 or 18 I almost died of an infection of the nerves of the heart

My heart was less then 20 beats a minute. Then it became fine.

I had a kidney stone removed at age 21.

I was French originally, I started not as an artist but as a mechanic, in the salt mines. I was in the French army during the French-Algerian war. I had a huge depression. I thought if I survived this I would survive anything. They shot me up with incredible drugs.

I have a low threshold for substances - smoke, drink, joints. Five mg knocks me out.

I used to be married. No children. I'm bi-sexual, I have lived for 5 years with a younger man. I miss women also which is a problem.

I've had big problem with my heart, since 18 years old. I twice had atrial fibrillation - 3 and 2 years ago. No coffee now as I'm worried about my heart.

Painting was a problem. I felt I did not do well enough. Now it's too late. I'm always that close to a breakthrough. Even though I showed in NY, Mexico and France, it is a problem. I don't know what else to do.

I got involved in mysticism, not a cult – SiddhaYoga – Guru Mai. For some years I was really involved. I tried meditation but became disenchanted. I was brought up Catholic but it's based on fear. On Sept 11, (I was born on the 12th) – for many years I wanted to make a will – I had an appointment at 10 a.m. on Wall Street. I went anyway. It was really fucking bad. (weeping). I changed and became bigoted. The Muslim religion is stupid, the stupidest religion in the world. I wasn't in really danger. I feel America is bad too.

I thought it was crazy to go there. Ninety-nine percent of policemen or firemen would have never gone in knowing it would fall. Heroes wouldn't have been heroes if they knew the building would go down. I wouldn't have gone there. Total panic, I really felt with tens of thousands of people. I kept going closer, like a mantra - I had to go to my appointment. We talked and I couldn't see out of the building anymore. A guy came in totally white or gray. I thought he was joking. Then it lifted and I went out. It was just very eerie. Different if you were there. I didn't want anyone to die. I had no idea it would affect me this way. When I think of it I feel fine but when I talk about it then it affects me. Afterwards I went to France to finish my will - in

October. In Europe the feeling was America deserved a little of this.

Twelve years ago my back pain got worse. I used to take paintings rolled up. Twelve large paintings. I was also not getting any sleep. No one helps you. I heard a sound in my back one time but I didn't feel anything for a year. Then I got a pain in the leg. I saw a chiropractor which made it worse it was so violent, I had three months in therapy. Then I had an operation. It relieved the pain in the legs. Now it comes and goes. There are times when it's bad, I cannot control my mid-section and need a brace. I feel I can walk fine if I walk backwards. I'm not depressed about my back, more about my heart, that I'll get a heart attack.

I've seen a heart specialist, it's skipping - atrial fibrillation. One thing in my head is when I was eighteen. *My heart was stopping until I lost consciousness, then it had to beat so strong I felt my head would explode. When my heart stopped it came from the legs up. It is imprinted on me for life. This wave came over me starting with the toes. My father died from a heart attack. Everyone in my family dies from the heart. I'm totally disassociated from myself, it's like a joke. Anyone with a nervous heart would have stopped. I felt I was not me anyone. I was gone. Everyone was looking. I was someone else - epinephrine. atropine, antibiotics. Then I cried and thought I would die. Today you put pacemakers in. Not then.*

Within an hour or so of sleeping I wake up. I dream of a film sped up one hundred times, passing through, it's really tiring. If I sleep too much I feel tired. Six hours is fine. I have a completely dry mouth, summer or winter. It's only when I sleep.

Dreams?

Nonsensical linking of imagery. Cut up one thousand films and put together one hundred times faster. I have normal dreams too.

One dream when I was young. Not sure if before or after my heart problem. It was prophetic. Two sections. I was in the woods and a guy came to talk to me. There is a road. I thought he was mute. There was a road beyond the trees. As soon as he said it I wanted to go. No one can find it. He took me on a path and it became colorized as we walked. Then he wasn't there. Still I wanted to find this road. The dream got faster and faster speeding by. But my foot was on a brand new road with a black top. Brand new. I remember I made a left turn, for ten feet. One hundred times faster. *On either side of the road on both sides was an infinite drop. The wind started to lift me off, it was totally dark.* There was no noise from the wind. I was unbelievably afraid. I tried to keep on the road. Roads to lead somewhere. *The moment was falling into eternity.* I grabbed a brush and it was somebody. Then I was on the road. At the end of dream was a castle, a straight road, up and down but straight. A guy in the castle said to me "how did you get here?"

He let me in and I sat down but wanted to go back. There was a fight over what meats and soups to give me. He gave me heavy weights so I can go back then he laughs demoniacally. It was a demonic laugh.

I've felt my life was a dream. I met this guy. I thought he was the man in the dream. I always wanted to go back. The end was always bad. I always felt my road was the art.

What is your art like?

Abstract. Expressionist, Van Gogh. Clean slate at tie of back. Figure linear expression of alphabet with bodies. Interesting, it had do with language. People on top of one another. Now back to doing abstract work.

Tell us about the comatose state?

It was nephritis? I lost consciousness. I had meningitis. I was foaming. Completely gone. Spinal fluid clear. Peeing albumin. So heavy in urine. They had to hold me up. Induced by uric acid in blood which swelled my brain. Idiots of the village. No antibiotics. I couldn't eat for two months, just rice in water.

I was born in 1939. My first memory was of planes going over bombing the shit out of the Germans. I was a skinny kid. My grandmother died of tremendous shock. She was head of the family, my mother's mother. I was 6 when she died.

What happened when you were ten years old?

Before the kidneys I was feeling bad. They had taken my appendix out. It was probably unnecessary. Probably was the kidney already.

They took out my tonsils. They gave me gas, it was a nightmare, I was not really under. I was in my own world. A giant was ripping out my throat. I didn't know what was happening. It could have lasted forever. I felt something warm, blood.

I had a breakdown during the army and was in a military hospital. There were guys with delirium, shell-shocked. I couldn't get up, I had no will to get up. I was really in a cell. They let me out for a few hours. A man told me if I don't get out I will be finished. I had lost the notion of time. I thought 3 seconds was one minute. I was given injections, there was no one to talk to - total chaos. I had pain in my head. I would wake up and my heart was beating a one hundred times a minute. I heard far away someone playing a piano and I felt the music was inside me. It was hard to get back on track. I returned to the mines. I would cry in the bathroom and then go back to work.

I really hated my work, comparing myself to my brothers who are gong to be big shots. The best thing was the episode with my heart. I ended up being a draftsman.

I fear losing control. When you die you lose control. I take my pill. Now there is less fear of sleeping. Getting to sleep is fine but I force myself not to sleep. If I don't take a pill it will be bad. It's a between state, not awake, not asleep. I'm already dreaming, not a normal dream. It's jumbled. I have fright about my heart beating. Things happen at night. Maybe it comes back to my grandmother dying at 3 a.m. I have episodes where I'm sure I'm going to die, or end up in St Vincent's emergency; seeing people who are really bad makes me feel better.

It's not imminent death, but unnatural sleep drains me. It's a state of being in-between. My mind is going berserk, it's incredibly tiring.

What is this in-between feeling?

When asleep time doesn't exist. I'm partially aware. My mind is going crazy. It's not dreaming and not a nightmare. Now it happens less often. One year ago I was totally fried and taken over by uncontrollable fear.

Do you have any phobias?

Walking without valium. In Peru I had altitude sickness and thought I would die. *Even in Mexico I don't like to be high up. I get sick from lack of oxygen, sick like hell. Supposedly you get sicker if have heart problems.*

Why did you go there

To visit friend in the jungle. Took yellow fever and malaria shot. Fucking building filled with medical tables. My father died when I was there. I think I went here because I knew. My heart went berserk. I went to hospital in Lima to bury my dad. I picked up transvestite and took him home. Went back three months later.

What happened in the army?

Half of it was in Germany. Until 1960 the French were still in Germany. Fine. Then Algiers was really bad, hospital, so bad. They put me with crazies.

What was it about it?

Chaos. More so then the French realized. Coup. Military. I was drafted. You didn't know. "If someone is against it step forward" no one stepped forward. *Worse in limbo, not doing anything, in a suspended state.*

Analysis

This case shows clear aspects of the remedy Tabacum. The history of nephritis with a comatose state is enough to consider this remedy. On top of that, his long-term heart pathology is also a key indicator for Tabacum. His very detailed and interesting dream shows aspect of the Tabacum state, especially the road with the infinite drop on either side, similar to the Native American stories of the abyss on the edge of the path and to the symptoms revealed in the proving. His connection to death is strong throughout his story, consistent with the theme of the proving and also his experience of an in-between state of consciousness was a key theme of the proving and was beautifully expressed by him.

Notes

Chapter One - The Substance, the Process and Its Human Connection

1. Pendell, Dale - *Pharmako/Poiea: Plant Power, Poisons, and Herbcraft*. Mercury House, San Francisco, CA, 1995, with a foreword by Gary Snyder. Reprinted with permission. **www.mercuryhouse.org/pendell.html**. P 38-39.
2. Ibid., P 34-35.
3. Narby, Jeremy - *The Cosmic Serpent: DNA and the Origins of Knowledge*. J.P. Tarcher, 1998. P. 30.
4. Ibid., P. 51.
5. Ibid., P. 61.
6. Ibid., P. 66.
7. Ibid., P. 178-179.

Chapter Two - A Brief History of Tobacco

1. Gately, Iain - *La Nicotiana, The Story of How Tobacco Seduced the World*. Scribner UK, 2002. P. 15-16.
2. Ibid., P. 18.
3. Ibid., P. 177-178.
4. Ibid., P. 35-36.
5. Ibid., P. 43.
6. Ibid., P. 82.

7. Ibid., P. 89.
8. Ibid., P. 98.
9. Ibid., P. 98.
10.Ibid., P. 126.
11.Ibid., P. 188.
12.Ibid., P. 205.
13.Ibid., P. 211.
14.Ibid., P. 233.
15.Ibid., P. 233-234.
16.Ibid., P. 277.
17.Ibid., P. 347.
18.Ibid., P. 355.
19.Ibid., P. 356.
20.Ibid., P. 358.

Chapter Three - Contemplations on the Impact of Tobacco

1. Vermeulen, Frans - *Prisma: The Arcana of materia Medica Illuminated.* Emryss bv Publishers, 2002. P. 1330.
2. Klein, Richard - *Cigarettes are Sublime.* Duke University Press, 1993.
3. Cunningham, Donna - *Further Dimensions of Healing Addictions.* Cassandra Press, California.
4. Klein, Richard - *Cigarettes are Sublime.* Duke University Press, 1993.
5. Ibid., P 36.
6. Ibid., P 40.
7. Ibid., P 43.
8. Ibid., P 43.
9. Ibid., P 36-37.
10.Ibid., P 35.
11.Ibid., P 137.
12.Ibid., P 141.
13.Ibid., P 143.
14.Ibid., P 144.

Chapter Four - Commentaries on Tobacco and the Proving

1. Pendell, Dale - *Pharmako/Poiea: Plant Power, Poisons, and Herbcraft.* Mercury House, San Francisco, CA, 1995, with a foreword by Gary Snyder. Reprinted with permission. **www.mercuryhouse.org/pendell.html**. P 38-39.
2. Cunningham, Donna - *Further Dimensions of Healing Addictions.* Cassandra Press, California.
3. Allen, Timothy Field - *Encyclopedia of Pure Materia Medica.* B. Jain Publishers LBI, New Delhi, p 472. Vol 9.
4. Johnstone, Paula (Lightening Woman) - **www.geocites.com/RainForest/Andes/1029/tobaccy.html**.

Chapter Five - Some Native American Uses of Tobacco and Their Associated Proving Symptoms

1. Wilbert, Johannes - *Tobacco and Shamanism in South America.* Yale University Press, New Haven. P 193-194.

Bibliography

Allen, Timothy Field - *Encyclopedia of Pure Materia Medica.* B. Jain Publishers LBI, New Delhi, p 472. Vol 9.

Colonial Virginia - *The Tobacco Economy.* **www.u-s-history.com/pages/h1154.html**

Croghan, Laura A. - *The Negroes to Serve Forever: The Evolution of Blacks's Life and Labor in Seventeenth-Century Virginia,* Masters Thesis, William and Mary, 1994, p.2.

Cunningham, Donna - *Further Dimensions of Healing Addictions.* Cassandra Press, California.

Duggie and Tony Spiritual Site - *Native American Tobacco Use.* **http://groups.msn.com/DuggieTonySpiritualSite/yourwebpage2.msnw**

Gately, Iain - La Nicotina, *The Story of How Tobacco Seduced the World.* Scribner UK, 2002.

Gray, John - *Straw Dogs: Thoughts on Humans and Other Animals.* Granta Books, 2003.

Herrick, Nancy - *Sacred Plants, Human Voices.* Hahnemann Clinic Publishing. 2003.

Houghton Mifflin, *Encyclopedia of North American Indians.* **http://college.hmco.com/history/readerscomp/naind/html/na_039200_tobacco.htm**

J.B. Fleming - *Neuro-Alchemy: Beta-Carbolines as Potentiating Agents.*

Johnstone, Paula - **www.geocites.com/RainForest/Andes/1029/tobaccy.html**

Klein, Richard - *Cigarettes are Sublime.*
Duke University Press, 1993

Morgan, Edmund S. - *American Slavery, American Freedom: The Ordeal of Colonial Virginia.*
Reprint, W.W. Norton, 1995. New York. 387 pp.

Native American Legends - *Symbolism of the Eagle Feather.* **http://home.online.no/~arnfin/native/lore/leg045.htm**

Narby, Jeremy - *The Cosmic Serpent: DNA and the Origins of Knowledge.*
J. P. Tarcher, April 1999, ppbk.

Nelson, Truman, ed. - *Documents of Upheaval: Selections from William Lloyd Garrison's* ***The Liberator****.*
Hill and Wang, 1966. New York.

Pendell, Dale - *Pharmako/Poiea: Plant Powers, Poisons, and Herbcraft.*
Mercury House, San Francisco, CA, 1995, with a foreword by Gary Snyder. Reprinted with permission. **www.mercuryhouse.org/pendell.html**

PortCities Bristol website - *Slavery Routes.*
www.discoveringbristol.org.uk/showTheme.php?sto_id=1

Randall, Prof. Vernellia R - *Tobacco, Health and the Law.*
Lesson 03, Tobacco and Native Americans. **http://academic.udayton.edu/health/syllabi/tobacco/lesson03.htm**

Rush, Dr. Benjamin - *Essays, Literary, Moral and Philosophical.*
Chapter on tobacco. 1798. pp 261-270.

Tobacco and Slavery in the Virginia Colony.
www.historypoint.org/education/teaching/history_backyard/print_tobacco_slavery_virginia_colonies.html

Tobacco Medicine.
http://www.geocities.com/RainForest/Andes/1029/tobaccy.html

Tobacco Use: a Cross-Cultural Comparison.
http://ethnobotany.yage.net/article1.html

Trevor Stone & Gail Darlington - *Pills, Potions and Poisons.*
Oxford University Press, 2000; ISBN: 19 850403 9

Vermeulen, Frans - *Prisma: the Arcana of Materia Medica Illuminated.*
Emryss bv Publishers, 2002.

Walsh, Lorena S. - *The Chesapeake Slave Trade: Regional Patterns, African Origins, and Some Implications.*
William and Mary Quarterly, January 2001

Wilbert, Johannes - *Tobacco and Shamanism in South America.*
Yale University Press, New Haven.

About the Author

Richard still smokes an occasional cigarette, mostly in company, or over a pint of beer in an English pub. He practices homeopathy in San Francisco, California and is Director of the Pacific Academy of Homeopathy. He can be reached at **www.richardpitt.com** or **homeopathy-academy.org**.